William Ellis

The American Mission in the Sandwich Islands

A Vindication and an Appeal, in Relation to the Proceedings of the

Reformed Catholic Mission at Honolulu

William Ellis

The American Mission in the Sandwich Islands
A Vindication and an Appeal, in Relation to the Proceedings of the Reformed Catholic Mission at Honolulu

ISBN/EAN: 9783744707749

Printed in Europe, USA, Canada, Australia, Japan

Cover: Foto ©ninafisch / pixelio.de

More available books at **www.hansebooks.com**

THE AMERICAN MISSION

IN

THE SANDWICH ISLANDS:

A VINDICATION AND AN APPEAL,

IN RELATION TO THE PROCEEDINGS OF

THE REFORMED CATHOLIC MISSION

AT HONOLULU.

By REV. W. ELLIS,

FORMERLY MISSIONARY IN THE SANDWICH ISLANDS; AND HONORARY MEMBER OF THE AMERICAN BOARD OF COMMISSIONERS FOR FOREIGN MISSIONS.

HONOLULU:
REPRINTED FROM THE LONDON EDITION, BY H. M. WHITNEY.
1866.

THE
SANDWICH ISLAND MISSIONS.

A FEW days after my return from Madagascar, I had the honor of meeting, at a banquet at the Mansion House, Emma, Queen Dowager of the Sandwich Islands, and of conversing with her Majesty and suite respecting friends whom I had known in her native land; and I have regretted that our ungenial climate obliged her Majesty to leave for a season, before I had any other opportunity of expressing the great pleasure which the occasion afforded me, not only on account of the high and just estimation in which her Majesty is held, but also on account of the hospitality and attention which I had received in Hawaii from my countryman, her honored ancestor, Mr. John Young.

During the short time that Queen Emma remained in England, meetings, at which her Majesty was present, were held in several parts of the country in favor of the Episcopate and English Mission recently sent out to Honolulu. It is well that her Majesty and suite were able to attend these meetings. They have afforded to all who have thus shared the privilege of personal intercourse with the illustrious visitor to our country, the most satisfactory evidence that could be desired of the influence under which her character has been formed, and the judgment and intelligence with which her education has been directed.

That a young, intelligent, and well-educated lady of highest rank in a remote and comparatively unfrequented country, should desire to visit a land of which report had, perhaps, often filled her youthful and wondering mind with visions of greatness and happiness, especially if to that land she could in part trace her own descent,* is very natural, and would of itself ensure a most cordial welcome. And if, in addition to these claims on our regard, such visitor were a Christian lady, belong-

---
*Mr. Young, grandfather to Queen Emma, was born in Liverpool about the year 1749.

ing to a small but interesting people, who, within scarcely more than a single generation, had been raised from a condition of rude, repulsive, and sanguinary idolatry to a state of intelligent refinement and Christian virtue, of which she herself was an example, her presence would call forth from every section of intelligent and Christian society amongst us, the kindest affection and sympathy.

Such is this Christian lady now amongst us; and if her visit to England should be rendered subservient to the advancement of that sacred work which, by God's blessing, has produced this great change in her native land, and should afford encouragement to the honored men who, through evil report and good report, have steadily labored on—some of them from the morning of life to the evening of age—in this holy enterprise, the satisfaction given by the visit of the Queen to our shores will be greatly enhanced.

On the contrary, it would be a result justly and deeply to be deplored, if this visit, through no intention on the part of our distinguished guest, but by reason of the mistakes of others, should be made the occasion of disturbing the peace of the Hawaiian churches, of introducing divisions and consequently weakness amongst them, as well as increasing the difficulties of those faithful men whose long and patient labors for the good of her people, Queen Emma herself must feel, entitle them to high and grateful esteem.

Elements of disturbance and hindrance to the peaceful and harmonious progress of the Gospel have been unnecessarily introduced to Hawaii by an Episcopal Mission called the Reformed Catholic Mission. But it will be still more deplorable if advantage is taken of the visit of Queen Emma to increase and persistently extend these sources of disquiet, by appealing to the sympathy which her presence so naturally excites, for the means of augmenting the force of the Reformed Catholic Mission in the Sandwich Islands. It seems desirable, therefore, to point out to the supporters of this and other Protestant missions the mistakes which prevail in relation to its origin, the grounds on which it is recommended, as well as the injurious effects which it is likely to produce, in the hope that the promoters of the Mission may be induced to reconsider the course on which they have entered before proceeding further.

If, in accordance with the wishes of the King and the Queen of Hawaii, who have expressed their decided preference for the Church of

England form of worship, friends in England should supply the means of gratifying her Majesty's wishes by the erection of a more architecturally symmetrical and attractive church in her distant island home than at present exists there, and to erect a suitable and durable monument to perpetuate the remembrance of the virtues of her departed husband, such exercise of their munificence would provide a lasting and valuable memorial of the generous sympathy of her friends, which all Protestants would regard with pleasure and approval.

But in no accounts that I have seen of the meetings held on behalf of the English Episcopal Mission at Honolulu, or in the publications in which its support has been advocated, has the source in which the scheme originated been correctly stated, or its continuance urged on existing and valid grounds. There has been on some occasions such a commingling of acknowledged facts with purely fictitious statements, such entire omission of some occurrences, and such a tendency to magnify others, as to make it scarcely possible that those to whom the statements were addressed should have received correct impressions on the subject. At the same time the evident love of right, and the desire to render justice to all parties concerned, are on some occasions so evident in the advocacy of the scheme, as to warrant the conclusion, that if the actual circumstances of the Hawaiians had been better known, the dignified and venerable Society which has so largely subsidized this scheme, and some of the distinguished individuals who have given the movement the just influence of their high position, might have hesitated before doing so, or may even yet deem it right to reconsider the true ground on which its claims rest, and the amount of support to which it is entitled.

It is from no wish to interfere in matters that do not concern me, but from a strong sense of duty towards the native Christians, among whom I many years ago resided,—to the faithful men with whom I formerly labored, as well as to the supporters of Protestant missions,—that with every feeling of good-will towards the projectors and supporters of the Episcopate and Mission in Hawaii, I ask, most respectfully, their serious attention to what appear to me to be some of the great mistakes connected with the appointment and persistent continuance of this Mission to the Sandwich Islands.

REPORTED APPLICATIONS FROM THE ISLANDS.

The promoters of the Reformed Catholic Mission affirm that the reasons for commencing that Mission extend back over a period of nearly eighty years, and a sort of historic and chivalrous charm is imparted to the enterprise by representing the non-compliance of the Government of England with a series of applications made by successive sovereigns of Hawaii as so many wrongs inflicted on the people which the Church of England is now called upon to redress. Captain Cook's sanction and support of their idolatry, by permitting their worship of himself, and receiving their victims offered in sacrifice—acts demanding unqualified condemnation—are justly described as one wrong; the refusal to send teachers in compliance with Kamehameha's request, made nearly twenty years afterwards, is a second; the like refusal of an application sent thirty years later by Kamehameha II., and his subsequent visit to England, is then stated; and after describing a conversation between our King, George IV., and the survivors of the lamented King and Queen, it is added, "At the same time the longing hopes of an eagerly expectant people for God's truth and ordinances was once more blasted; and history, which is no courtier, will set down the lofty indifference of George IV. to their pious aspirations as another of those wrongs done to the Hawaiian people for which England and its Church are at this moment called upon to make reparation."*

Whether or not these wrongs were ever inflicted we now proceed to inquire. In the "Colonial Church Chronicle," it is stated that Vancouver, who visited the Sandwich Islands in 1792, when conversing with the King, "remonstrated with him as to the folly of idolatry, and spoke to him of the one true Lord, the Creator, the Ruler, the Redeemer, and the Judge of all mankind," and adds that these words "were not spoken in vain. The King's own mind must have been strongly impressed to have prompted the request, so earnestly urged by him, for teachers from England, and that formal cession of his Kingdom to Great Britain which Vancouver accepted on behalf of his Sovereign." After stating that the cession was not accepted, the writer continues, "The request for teachers to be sent from England was equally disregarded;" and a few lines farther on, speaking of the King's death, he adds—seemingly with a

* "Colonial Church Chronicle," 1865, p. 353.

view to show the influence of Vancouver's words on his mind—"Kamehameha, with no more real belief in them possibly than Socrates had in a like performance, did homage to the gods," &c. And again, when adverting to the abolition of idolatry by the successor of the deceased sovereign, it is observed, "It is clear that the new King and the old high priest perfectly understood one another; that their conversation touching the idols, which is on record, had not for its object to draw out each other's mind, but to shift the burden of the first decisive avowal from the one to the other. The hope of getting teachers from England had never been abandoned. It was the religion of England to be brought from England by the long-promised teachers that all along fed the national expectation. The Hawaiians were looking with an eager eye for 'the Church of the future,' to be sent to them, according to Vancouver's engagement, from England."*

Inferences, conclusions, revelations of the state of mind, &c., among the people, more or less connected with these quotations, which occupy a number of pages of this appeal on behalf of the Mission published in the above-mentioned periodical, are all very interesting, but without the slightest reference to the authority on which they are made. I do not say there is no authority for these statements, only that the writer does not adduce any; and that no evidence of any such authority has ever come under my notice. But there is evidence, clear and strong, which renders it highly improbable that the remonstrance, if offered, produced any impression on the King's mind, or that Vancouver's promise of teachers was ever made.

Vancouver relates very circumstantially, in the narrative of his visits to Hawaii in 1793 and 1794, his conversations with Kamehameha, many of which related to the idolatry of the country, the pagan rites, and priests; and he describes the worship and ceremonies within the temple, some of which he attended, and took part in the services,† but he never, throughout the whole narrative, makes the slightest allusion to his mention of the folly of idolatry, or of the worship of the one true Lord, &c.

I landed in April, 1822, on the shore of Kealakeakua Bay, where

---
* "Colonial Church Chronicle," 1865, pp. 349-50.

† Vancouver did speak to the King and priests when in the idol temple with them, but it was rather in confirmation of their idolatry than otherwise. He requested that the oxen and sheep he had brought might be *tabooed*, as a means of preserving them. (Vancouver's Voyage, vol. iii., pp. 52-3.

Captain Cook was killed, and in which Vancouver lay at anchor during his stay at Hawaii. I met Mr. Young the same day, and the pleasure of the meeting appeared to be mutual. We were very frequently together during the succeeding five months. We often spoke of the state of the Hawaiians as well as of the people I had left in Tahiti. He said that when he heard there were English missionaries at Tahiti, he often wished we had come to Hawaii as well. He also talked of Vancouver's visit, and the ship he helped them to build; but I have no recollection nor memorandum of his ever mentioning Vancouver's promise to send teachers from England, which it seems natural that he would have done when English teachers at Tahiti and their absence from Hawaii were the subjects of conversation.

On the other hand, Vancouver's narrative affords abundant evidence that the dread of the gods exercised the strongest influence over the minds of the people, and that the power of the priests, if not supreme, was next to that of the King. At that time both were combined in one person, Kamehameha being King and priest.

The account of the cession of the Islands to England is circumstantially given. The object of the King in making such cession, which was declined by our Government, appears to have been to secure the protection of England against aggression from other nations. Several speeches were delivered by the high chiefs, and from all these it was understood that "in their *religion*, government, and domestic economy, no interference was to take place; that Kamehameha, the chiefs, and the priests, were to officiate with the same authority as before in their respective stations, and that no alteration in these particulars was in any degree thought of or intended."*

I may be mistaken; but in the absence of all evidence of any application of the King for teachers from England, and in the face of the stipulations in an act so important as the public formal cession of their country, guarding their religion as well as government from all interference, I find it difficult to conceive, without evidence, that any application for teachers was ever made by the King, or any promise given by Vancouver.

As there is at present so much reason for doubt respecting the promise, it is needless to say anything about its effects—about the Hawai-

* Vancouver, vol. iii., pp. 56-7.

ians "looking with an eager eye to 'the Church of the future' to be sent to them, according to Vancouver's engagement, from England." But as that supposed engagement is one of the reasons assigned for sending out the Reformed Catholic Mission, it may be added, that there is mournfully conclusive evidence that Vancouver's remonstrance, if ever uttered, had made no lasting or salutary impression on the King's mind, and that he died a heathen, and charged his successor and his associates to support the dark and terrible idolatry of the country.

In the disposition of the Kingdom Kamehameha bequeathed to his son Liholiho the government of the country, but devolved on him and on Kekuaokelani,* his first cousin, and the other high officers and priests, the care of the gods and the support of the tabu. When the new King meditated the abolition of the tabu, one of the priests said no evil would follow;† but most of the other priests, and the prince to whom also the support of the old religion had been confided, were of a different opinion, and took up arms to avenge the gods. In the battle at Kuamoo which followed, the prince and his heroic wife Manono fought and fell side by side, and were buried in the same grave.‡ This battle destroyed the idolatry of the country, the first step towards which was the abolition of the tabu.

In appeals made on behalf of the Reformed Catholic Mission during the past year,§ it is stated that the application for English teachers made by the King through Vancouver was repeated by his successor in a letter to George IV., sent in acknowledgment of the present of a ship in 1822. I had arrived at Hawaii with that ship, had remained there five months, and was returning for a very short time to the Southern Islands with the Captain who had presented the ship, and I was perfectly acquainted with the contents of the letter, which was written the day before our departure. That letter contained no allusion to any former promise, nor application for teachers from England. The King acknowl-

---

* Signifying the God of the Heavens, which would lead to the inference that he was also a priest.

† Mr. Young, who accompanied Messrs. Tyerman and Bennett and myself to the house at which the banquet took place, described the proceedings in which the guests, instead of appearing to him to have expected the violation of the tabu, were struck with horror and consternation. One of the Queens, at least, said the King had informed them of his intention.

‡ An account of this battle was published in 1828. in the "Tour in Hawaii," pp. 103-10, and in the Journal of Messrs. Tyerman and Bennett, vol. i., p. 379.

§ "Tract on Hawaiian Church Mission," p. 3. "Colonial Church Chronicle," p. 352.

edged the receipt of the present; announced the conquest of the entire group of islands by his father; their bequest to himself; and he then begged leave to place them under the protection of George IV., expressing confidence in his Majesty's wisdom and judgment. The closing paragraph of his letter is as follows :—" The former idolatrous system has been abolished in these Islands, as we wish the Protestant religion of your Majesty's dominions to be practiced here. I hope your Majesty will deem it fit to answer this as soon as convenient, and your Majesty's counsel and advice will be thankfully received."

The wish for an answer referred not at all to the Protestant religion, which was then practiced in the Islands, but to what weighed far more heavily on the King's mind—the refusal of England to accept the cession of the Islands made to Vancouver, and to what was the great desire of the King, chiefs, and people, as was often expressed to myself, the guaranteed protection of England, which the King in that letter so suppliantly begged from George IV.

It is farther asserted, in support of the great mistake about this letter, that no answer having been received to his request for teachers, the King resolved to come to England himself, and that " his object was, as there is every reason to suppose, to take back with him an English Church Establishment." Here again there is no evidence that this formed any part of the King's purpose in making the visit, or that it was ever mentioned by him while he lived, or by his companions after his decease. But there is evidence that one, if not the chief object sought by Kamehameha in coming to England, was to secure, by personal application to the King of England, the protection of his country by the English Government.

This King and his Queen sickened and died before they had any opportunity of stating their object, or even seeing the King of England. The chiefs of their suite afterwards saw his Majesty at Windsor, and on their return to the Islands reported the advice which George IV. had given them. Boki, the brother of the then regent of the Kingdom, said, "That when he inquired of the King whether preachers were good men, his Majesty answered, 'Yes; and they are men to make others good. I have always some of them by me; for chiefs are not wise like them. We in England were once like the people in your Islands; but this kind of teachers came, and taught our fathers; and now you see what we are.' And again, 'You and your people must take good heed to the missionaries; for they were sent to enlighten you, and do you good. They came not for secular purposes, but by a Divine command to teach you the Word of God. The people would therefore all do well to attend to instruction, and to forsake stealing, drunkenness, war, and everything evil, and to live in peace.' "*

Kekuanaoa, the venerable father of the present King, and still a member of the Hawaiian Church, stated, "This is what we heard of the charge of King George: 'Return to Kamehameha III., and tell him *I will protect his country.* To any evil from abroad I will attend. The evils within the country are not my concern, but the evils from without.' "†

With these chieftains and two others, the officers of the London Missionary Society had several interviews. The chiefs gave the strongest assurances of the continued support of their Government to the missionaries then in the Sandwich Islands, and added their request that another missionary might be sent out with them to be my fellow-laborer in Hawaii, as stated in the subjoined extract from a letter addressed to me, and dated "London, September 8th, 1824:"

"The chiefs, Boki in particular, having expressed a desire that a missionary should accompany them on their return to the Sandwich Islands, and Lord Byron, Commander of H. M. S. *Blonde,* having kindly intimated his readiness to take out a missionary in that vessel, the Directors, considering it desirable that you should have a colleague, deemed it their duty to appoint a missionary to Hawaii." It having at length been found that the ship was crowded both as to persons and baggage, Mr. Pitman, the missionary appointed, went afterwards in another vessel.

Thus it appears that the Hawaiian Government was satisfied with the Mission already established in the country, and desired it to be strengthened rather than supplanted by another. The whole of the circumstances which have been brought under review seem to show that the new Mission cannot be justified on the grounds of any application to Vancouver, any letter from Liholiho, his son, or by his visit to this country.

* Bingham's History, quoted in "North American Review," No. lviii., p. 59.
† Anderson's "Hawaiian Islands," p. 62.

It now remains to consider the last application said to have been made by the late King, Kamehameha IV. The scheme for sending out a Bishop and Church of England missionaries did not, according to the evidence we possess, originate in the Sandwich Islands, but in England. The only valid reasons which I have seen for any movement in this direction, appear to be the want of a clergyman of their own communion felt by members of the Church of England, or of the Episcopalian Churches of America residing in Honolulu, and the wish of the King, who preferred that form of worship, and desired that it should be introduced to his capital.

It would have given pleasure to the ministers of the Island churches, to their supporters in America, and to the friends of Protestant missions generally, had these just and reasonable desires been complied with. It was all the applicants asked for. No desire for a Bishop, no want of a Mission appears, according to the testimony of the late chief Minister of the King, to have been felt at Honolulu, when this application from the Islands was received. That application was in part officially addressed to myself.

Early in the year 1860, I received two letters, dated respectively on the 29th of February and the 13th of March of that year. The former of these was from Dr. Armstrong, President of the Board of Public Instruction in the Sandwich Islands, stating that there were at Honolulu a number of persons and a few families, either members of the Episcopal Church, or partial thereto, who had long desired the services of an Episcopalian minister to "break to them the bread of life;" that the King of Hawaii had directed his Minister for Foreign Affairs to authorize Manly Hopkins, Esq., his Charge d'Affaires in London, to guarantee to a suitable clergyman of the Episcopal Church an annual salary of one thousand dollars, and had offered, besides, ground for the site of a church. Dr. Armstrong also stated that he applied to me at the request of several Episcopalians, who wished to secure as their minister "a man of Evangelical sentiments, respectable talents, and most exemplary Christian life," mentioning a clergyman who had been recommended to them, and whom they would cordially welcome, at the same time communicating his address, and pointing out the steps which he wished me to take.

Dr. Armstrong stated that he applied to me because I had resided in the Islands, had been associated with the missionaries there, and

THE SANDWICH ISLAND MISSIONS. 13

knew the people and the kind of clergyman most likely to do good there.

The second letter was from the late R. C. Wyllie, Esq., the King's Minister for Foreign Affairs, and to whom I had been known in the Sandwich Islands. He states that Dr. Armstrong's letter, which he enclosed, was on the subject of the establishment in that capital of an Episcopal Church; that the King and Queen preferred that form of worship, and the King believed that an Episcopal Church there, besides supplying a want long felt by many British and American families, would operate beneficially in narrowing the broad antagonism existing between the Calvinistic and Catholic creeds, and promoting brotherly feeling between the clergy of both. He added that by the orders of the King he had written to Mr. Manly Hopkins, who would communicate to me what further information I might desire.*

I lost no time in waiting on Mr. Hopkins, who appeared surprised at my having been written to; said he was acquainted with the wish for a clergyman expressed in the letters I had received, but that it was intended to send out a Bishop accompanied by some clergymen, and he handed me a printed statement or appeal on behalf of this object. I expressed my regret that such an intention had been formed, and stated my opinion that the object sought by the writers of the letters would be more effectually secured by compliance with their distinctly expressed wishes.

The explicit statement of Dr. Armstrong that a single clergyman was desired for Honolulu, and the reference which he makes in his letter to me to the desire of the Episcopalians to detain among them one of two clergymen who spent a short time at Honolulu on their way to British Columbia, accord with the statement of Mr. Wyllie that a Church of England was wanted for the capital, and his repeated affirmation that the King did not desire the services of a Bishop.† The silence of Mr. Hopkins as to any application having been made for a Bishop while informing me that it was intended to send one out; the statement in the paper which he placed in my hand, and the speech of that gentleman at Chelmsford, on the occasion of Queen Emma's visit there, when he stated, "It was thought that the work of the English Church would fail

---

* See Appendix A.
† "Patriot," November 16th, 1865.

without an Episcopal head, and accordingly a Bishop was sent out from England, and three earnest and zealous clergymen accompanied him"—all these facts force upon my mind the conviction that no request for a Bishop was included in the original application from the Islands; and that the request actually made by the members of the Church of England for an Evangelical clergyman has not been complied with.

As I considered that the settlement of an Evangelical clergyman at Honolulu would be a means of great good there, I was ready to aid its accomplishment; but I never deemed it desirable to take any steps beyond recommending it. I placed the documents which I had received in the hands of the officers of the Church and Continental Society, who communicated with the Bishop of London on the subject, and received his lordship's approval, but failed to engage a suitable clergyman until it had been decided by the Bishop of Oxford and others to send out a Bishop; and before this decision was carried into effect, I had left England for Madagascar. Since my return, I find it stated that the King of Hawaii did write for a Bishop and clergymen of the English Church. But this seems to have been an after-thought, whether originating in the royal mind or elsewhere. Such subsequent application cannot, therefore, be regarded as furnishing the reason why a Mission was determined upon in England, and a Bishop was sought for before it had been received. The fact seems to be, that the gentlemen with whom the scheme originated viewed the application for a single clergyman to meet an acknowledged want as furnishing an occasion for establishing an Episcopate and commencing a Mission in the Sandwich Islands, and took measures accordingly.

A writer in the "Colonial Church Chronicle" states very circumstantially, that "It was towards the close of the year 1859, in the fifth year of his reign, that Kamehameha IV. addressed to the Queen of England, and through his Ministers to the Archbishop of Canterbury, the request that a Mission of the Church of England should be sent out to Honolulu." The writer does not, however, give any copy or extracts of these letters, nor the dates at which they were either written or received. The statements respecting these requests are not explicit. Some circumstances connected with them certainly require explanation. For instance, the letters from the King's Minister to myself, arrived in less than two months after their dates in 1860. How could it then occur, if these letters had been written in 1859, that towards the end of 1860 his Grace the Archbishop of Canterbury remained in perfect ignorance of any such request having been made to him? In the meantime an English journal had announced that there was an idea of introducing Anglicanism, and if possible its Episcopate, into the Sandwich Islands, and that an effort was being made by Mr. Manly Hopkins, in concert with the Society for the Propagation of the Gospel, to accomplish this object. That announcement being copied into a Sandwich Island newspaper, which was forwarded to America, the American Missionary Society wrote to the Archbishop of Canterbury, asking his Grace to use his influence to dissuade the venerable Society for the Propagation of the Gospel, from extending its operations to the Sandwich Islands. The following is the honored Primate's reply:

"LAMBETH PALACE, September 28, 1860.

"REVEREND SIR:—In consequence of the letter dated 3d instant, which I had the honor of receiving from you, I have made inquiry on the subject to which it refers; and I find it to be quite true, that certain individuals have formed themselves into a committee, for the purpose of taking advantage of the proposal of the King of Hawaii, and with the ultimate view of establishing a Bishop on the Polynesian Islands.

" The subject does not originate with the Society for Propagating the Gospel, to which it has not been hitherto proposed. And it is altogether untrue, that the Archbishop encourages the plan, of which, in fact, he was ignorant until your letter arrived.

" Should an attempt be made to connect this object with the Society for Propagating the Gospel, I shall think it my duty to lay your letter before the persons who chiefly administer its affairs; and I shall be truly sorry if any circumstances shall occur calculated to create jealousy between parties who have the same great end in view—an object which would be counteracted by collision, in the same degree as it may be promoted by co-operation.

" With high respect for the Society to which you belong, and much thankfulness for the work which God has enabled it to effect,

"I remain, Reverend Sir, your faithful servant,

"J. B. CANTUAR.

" *To the Secretary of the Board of Missions.*"*

---
* This letter is given in the interesting and valuable account of the Rev. Dr. Anderson, Foreign Secretary of the American Missionary Society, entitled "The

This evidence will scarcely be impugned, and viewed in connection with the language employed in justifying the Hawaiian Episcopate, which represents it as having originated in the spontaneous wish of the King, it can scarcely fail, in the judgment of unprejudiced men, to vitiate the grounds on which the whole scheme has been reared.

THE LIMITED FIELD SUFFICIENTLY OCCUPIED.

If the evangelization of the Hawaiian Islands were now to be commenced, a Bishop and six clergymen would not, considering the claims of other parts of the world, be a very disproportionally small staff of laborers for a beginning in so diminutive a field. How unreasonably excessive then must such a number of additional missionaries be under existing circumstances!

But this small field has been long and ably occupied by agents of the American Board of Commissioners for Foreign Missions—a Missionary Society organized at first chiefly among the descendants of the Pilgrim Fathers in the New England States, but now receiving voluntary support from Christians in thirty-seven States of the Union, and governed by a Board of Members residing in twenty-two of these States. This Society sent out in 1819 a well-appointed Mission comprising, besides liberally educated clergymen accredited by the authorities of the churches to which they belonged, a physician, assistants, and school-masters, a printer and press, and an agriculturist. A second band, sent out a year or two afterwards, increased the number of ordained and equally well-qualified clergymen, and added a superintendent of secular affairs to the Mission.

I knew these men, some of whom still continue in the field. My knowledge of them extends over more than forty years. I lived and labored with some of them on most intimate terms, often under the same roof. We studied the language together, and labored unitedly in the schools, in preaching, in journeying. I was associated with them in many of the new, difficult, and critical positions in which a recently planted Mission almost invariably finds itself placed, while feeling its way among a people ignorant, proud, suspicious, barbarous, and all but nominally heathen. And my testimony concerning these missionaries

Hawaiian Islands, their Progress and Condition," published after an official visit to the American Missions in the Sandwich Islands in 1863.

is that, for the work they had undertaken, they were well-qualified men, worthy of their training and of their ancestry. I often marked and admired their unobtrusive piety, and their persevering conscientious attention to all the great objects of their Mission, their simple style of living, the absence among them of self-seeking and self-indulgence, and their self-consecration to their sacred work. Such were the first missionaries to Hawaii, and, according to all reliable testimony, there is no reason to suppose that their successors have been less qualified for their work, or less entitled to the esteem of all good men. To call these missionaries, some of whom had devoted eight or nine years to training for their work, a band of "uneducated and narrow-minded men," is to insult the intelligent portion of the American people, and to libel the educational institutions of their country; but it will inflict no injury on the missionaries in the estimation of any who are acquainted with their labors, or capable of appreciating their worth.

I do not speak of these men as perfect: nothing human is so. They have doubtless their failings as well as others, and are as liable to mistakes in the prosecution of a great object. They have had to acquire their experience under many difficulties; but, notwithstanding this, all unprejudiced men will regard their labors as having conduced, in an eminent degree, to the well-being of the Hawaiians, both for the present life and for that which is to come.

Without at present adverting to the external improvements which are visible among the Hawaiians, the numbers who, notwithstanding all defections, have, through the labors of these missionaries, become intelligent and earnest Christians, showing their sincerity by long-continued, irreproachable conduct, have not, in my opinion, been surpassed in any Mission field; while the extent to which the influence of Christianity is diffused in different degrees amongst large portions of the entire community warrants the great majority of the Sandwich Islanders being regarded as, in the usual acceptation of the term, a Christian people.

It is scarcely conceivable that anything else than want of accurate acquaintance with the extent to which Christianity prevailed among the Sandwich Islanders, could have allowed a number of distinguished Christian gentlemen to enter upon such a work of supererogation as that of sending out so large a Mission to so small a field, so well supplied with Christian ministers, whose labors had been so eminently successful. Evidence was at hand, and it is of the suppression, excepting in some gratifying instances, of the testimony in favor of the good already accomplished that I complain, as tending to produce mistakes respecting the nature of the new Mission to the Sandwich Islands, for that object does not seem to be to convert the heathen to Christ, so much as to draw away members from long-established Presbyterian and Congregational churches to a section of the Church of England.

Many, however, have been led to suppose that there are still heathen to convert. Mr. Manly Hopkins, at Chelmsford, combating objections on account of the small population of the Islands, exclaims—" Good heavens! seventy thousand not to be saved!" And the Bishop of London also appears, I am persuaded unintentionally, to have fallen into the mistake of supposing that there are numbers of heathens in Hawaii. In a speech delivered at Wells, on the occasion of Queen Emma's visit to that city, his lordship, after specifying some of the claims of the Bishop of Honolulu, thus continued :—" He is also a missionary Bishop, with a great Mission work to perform. The accounts show that there is great room for bringing the heathen to the knowledge and the love of God," &c. Many others are no doubt of the same opinion. There is reason to believe that in the judgment of a large number of members of the Church of England, as well as of other communions, the sending out of a Bishop and three, or, as is now proposed, six English clergymen to Hawaii, can only be justified on the supposition that there is a large heathen or non-Christian population, which the American missionaries have failed to bring under Christian instruction, or who have relapsed into heathenism. But that such opinion is well founded, there is no reliable evidence.

Bishop Staley has put forward the statement that there are more than 20,000 unevangelized natives in the Islands, and this statement has been accepted as one of the chief grounds on which the scheme has been advocated. Bishop Staley quotes, as his authority, a local newspaper which gives the following statement:

68,000 Hawaiians (the whole population.)
20,000 professing Protestants.
20,000 Romanists.
3,000 Mormons.
25,000 unconnected with any creed.*

---
* Bishop Staley's Journal, p. 47.

The amount of the whole population as here given is correct, but the other numbers must have been derived from erroneous data. One or two of the items, however, bear some resemblance to the report of the division of the people in 1862, published by the Roman Catholic Bishop, and given in the "Propaganda Fide." In that statement the Romanists are put down at 23,000.
The heretics, 23,000.
Infidels, 23,000.*

Evidence is available, and there are documents at hand by which the above statement of Bishop Staley may be tested and explained, though we may not be informed of the data on which it has been arranged. The American missionaries publish their annual reports, which contain exact lists of the numbers of the Christian Church "in regular standing;" that is, of communicants; stating also the numbers suspended from communion, and the numbers baptized each year. The statistics of each island and each missionary district are given in detail, and, being published on the spot, may be regarded as unquestionable. Now, in the returns for the year 1863, the number of *communicants* was that stated above—viz, 20,000. Any one acquainted with missions may calculate the proportion of children and of non-communicants in a Mission comprising 20,000 communicants. The Annual Report of the American Society for 1865, which has just come to hand, gives the number in regular standing as 17,521, adding: "There is a gradual decrease in the numbers of church members, owing to the excess of deaths and excommunications above the admissions." The reduction in the number of church members has by no means kept pace, during many past years, with the decrease of the population in the Islands.

The missionaries, themselves members of the Congregational and Presbyterian churches of America, exercise much care in the reception of converts from among the heathen to the communion of the Hawaiian churches. Only those are admitted who give evidence of having, by the influence of the Holy Spirit, become partakers of a new and spiritual

---

* Romanist statistics are not always reliable in matters connected with their own adherents, or those of their opponents. As the population has diminished since 1860, when it was 68,000, and there is no reason to suppose that the adherents of the Catholics at all approximate to the numbers they have given, the figures here stated must be incorrect. The largest number of adherents to the Romanists that I have seen stated by any of the American missionaries is as one to ten of the Protestants. This only refers to one province or island.

life; and none are allowed to remain communicants whose conduct is not such as the New Testament enjoins. Deviations from this rule, repeated or continued, are always, when known, considered valid reasons for exclusion from their fellowship. In regard to Christian attainments and consistency of life, there is no reason to suppose that the Christians of Hawaii are, in these respects, inferior to the communicants in other Mission churches, or that their numbers are proportionally fewer.

In the most prosperous missions the communicants generally amount to one in three.* In ordinary cases they are one in four or five. Taking therefore the lowest number of communicants, that of last year—viz, 17,521—and supposing those in "regular standing" to be one in three, though, as those excommunicated are still cared for, the entire number of natives under the care of the American missionaries, including communicants, children, sick persons, and catechumens, would be 52,563 or 60,000 in 1862, the year in which the Bishop and clergymen arrived. The decrease of the communicants from deaths and excommunications has not, according to the statements of the missionaries, kept pace with the decrease of the population. This, according to the rate of decrease since the last census—viz, 562 annually—would reduce the native population in 1865, the year for which the number of communicants has been given, to 64,274. Deducting from these the number under the care of the American missionaries, there would remain 10,711.

The Catholics state that they have 18 European priests, 12 Catechist brothers, 80 religious pupils, 10 nuns, 28 decent chapels, 30 ditto of straw, and 50 schools. Suppose the number of their native adherents, instead of being as they state, 23,000, should not amount to half that number, say only to 10,000, there would remain 711 souls uncared for; but their spiritual wants would be amply met by the labors of Rev. Mr. Damon, American chaplain for seamen, who preaches in English at Honolulu, and the clergyman whose services the friends of the Church of England had desired.

* Dr. Mullens' "Statistical Tables for India and Ceylon in 1862," give—Native Christians, 153,816; communicants, 30,249; making the communicants nearly one in five of the professed Christians.

The American Board only publish the numbers of communicants and average attendants on public worship. The statistics for India and Ceylon for last year give the number of communicants as one in three to the average number of their congregations; and as a number of young children, sick persons and others must always be absent from public worship, the number of native Christians must be greater than that above stated. In the missions with which I have been personally connected, the communicants have been as one in four or five of the adherents to Christianity.

In the foregoing statement, the 23,000 infidels which find a place in the Catholic statistics are not included, because, excepting the Mormons, whatever their numbers may be, the list of those to whom the Romanists apply this designation, though not baptized, are, according to the testimony of Dr. Anderson,* more or less connected with the Protestant congregations, as infants, young persons, members of families, attendants at public worship, &c.

There may be, and doubtless is, some amount of superstition still lingering among portions of the people in remote places, where its most frequent manifestation is connected with causes producing sickness, or the administering of native nostrums for the cure of disease, as still prevails in some parts of our own country. There may be some lingering heathen belief and concealed heathen practices in some places and at different times among a small number of the people; but Dr. Anderson states that "there is not a single avowed heathen" or known worshiper of idols throughout the whole group of the Islands.

The selection of Honolulu for the commencement of an English Mission is a still more manifest aggression upon an existing church. The population of this place was, when the last census was taken, 14,310— viz, 1,639 foreigners, and 12,671 natives. There are already at Honolulu, and connected with the American Mission, two large native churches, one of them built of stone, capable of accommodating 2,500 hearers. The number of communicants connected with these churches was stated in the returns for last year at 3,367. Supposing the communicants to be one in three of those under the care of the missionaries, there are 10,101 native Christians. There is also one chapel in which the services are in English, besides a Roman Catholic Cathedral. Here then there is ample church room for the entire population, even at the most crowded season of the year; nevertheless, at this place it is proposed to erect another cathedral, which is required neither by Protestants nor Catholics, and which can only be filled by emptying existing churches.

Such are the conclusions to which the only reliable statistics of the Islands inevitably lead. The Government census may be depended upon as correct. The statistics of the American Mission, considering the minuteness and detail with which they are given, the length of time dur-

* Anderson's "Hawaiian Islands," p. 367.

ing which they have been regularly published year by year at the capital, under the eyes of the Government, and open to the criticism of the foreign residents, must remain unquestioned. No other statistics of the religious state of the people, whether derived from the Romanist Bishop, or copied from the pages of a local newspaper, can be equally reliable.

These statistics show most clearly, and beyond all questioning, that, so far as the religious state of the people is concerned, while the appointment of an English clergyman, as in the first instance solicited, would have supplied an acknowledged want, and would have gratified the preference of the Sovereign and his amiable Queen, as well as encouraged the faithful men who had long pre-occupied the ground, the sending out of an English Bishop and a staff of clergymen was an unnecessary and unjustifiable intrusion upon another Christian Society's field of labor. There is in fact no "great missionary work," or any truly missionary work, at all for the Bishop to do, and he can gather no missionary flock without first drawing away the sheep from another shepherd's fold.

REASONS ASSIGNED FOR SENDING OUT A NEW MISSION INVALID.

To send forth a Christian Mission to a heathen country is a simple act of Christian duty for which there is Divine authority and apostolic example. It admits of no doubt, and allows of no questioning. But to send forth such a Mission to a Christian country, is to enter upon a different course. For such a proceeding there is neither Divine authority, nor apostolic example. St. Paul expressly declared that, in prosecuting his great missionary work, he had striven "not to preach the Gospel where Christ was named, lest he should build upon another man's foundation."*

The promoters of a Mission to a people already Christians, place themselves in a wrong position at the beginning, excite doubt as to there being any necessity for their work, and questioning as to the end proposed. If Holy Scripture, the only true foundation of the Protestant faith, be the basis of their common belief, their acknowledged rule of life, and the standard by which their claim to discipleship is to be decided, doubts as to the necessity for such a Mission must be greatly strengthened.

A Mission to the heathen commends itself to every Christian's approval, and needs no justification. But the originators of a Mission to

* Rom. xv. 20.

a Christian people find it necessary to adduce reasons for entering such a field, and evidence that those reasons are sound. Such appears to have been the position of the gentlemen who formed themselves into a committee for sending "the Reformed Catholic Mission"* to the Sandwich Islands, and sustaining it there. They have sent out the Mission, and now find it necessary to show that it was required, and that their proceedings are justified.

The first reason alleged, I have already disposed of, by showing that the Mission did not originate in any application from the Kings of Hawaii, and was not required by a heathen or non-Christian population in the Islands, I proceed to notice the reasons said to arise out of the supposed defective qualifications of the missionaries, their mismanagement, and the effects of their labors.

The past history of the Hawaiian Islands, according to the observation of independent witnesses, affords abundant evidence that the American missionaries have accomplished a great work in the evangelization of these Islands. Few modern missions have, in an equally short period, been more successful than the Hawaiian Mission, and none have met with a larger measure of misrepresentation respecting the results of their labors.

A few, chiefly anonymous, writers in America have made injurious statements, which have been unhappily adopted in England, to justify the intervention of the new Mission. Yet, when examined, these depreciating statements rest upon nothing more than the lamentations of faithful ministers of Christ over the slow progress of their people in Christian attainments, and the disappointment which, in common with

---

* This is the name given to the Mission at home, and by the Bishop in the Islands. What is meant is not apparent. It cannot mean catholic in charity, as comprehending all who hold the Scriptural doctrines of Protestantism, for these the Presbyterian and Congregational churches in America to which the missionaries belong most surely believe; yet the members of this Reformed Catholic Mission refused to allow to the American missionaries their standing as clergymen which is accorded to them in their own country, and declined to unite with them in a meeting for prayer, because they did not regard "episcopal ordination as of Divine appointment." The Americans, much to their credit, manifested a readiness to co-operate, as far as possible, with the members of the newly-arrived Mission; but how their advances were met we learn from Mr. W. D. Alexander, who, in replying to Bishop Staley's pastoral, declares that "the overbearing and intolerant spirit which the Bishop and his presbyters displayed, and their apparent determination to ride rough-shod over their predecessors, and to use the influence and patronage of the Government to further their schemes, put all co-operation out of the question."

missionaries in other fields, they often have to suffer, over the tares which everywhere grow with the wheat in "the Kingdom of God."

Such unfair representations, grounded on what are called the confessions of the missionaries, is a favorite practice with men of the world, and with Romish writers, against Protestant missions, but is unjustifiable in those who profess their adherence to Scriptural truth. It may be well, however, to meet these aspersions by a brief review of the work of the Mission, and by counter testimony.

It is needless to attempt any refutation of the anonymous imputations cast upon the Mission, often by men whose ignorance, profligacy and vice disqualify them for giving evidence in such a case. I will therefore only briefly notice some of the disparaging statements which a too easy credulity has induced men of character and station to adopt and repeat, to the injury of this Mission.

It is acknowledged that the missionaries are earnest and faithful men, of pure and blameless life, that their creed is Scriptural, and their labors abundant; but they are charged with not being qualified for their work, with not having gained the affections of the people, and having no hold on their hearts. Hence, it is asserted by the Committee of the Catholic Reformed Mission, that "among their nominal converts there still exists a heathen belief, and heathen practices thinly veiled under a superficial Christianity."*

Connected with the purpose for which it is used, the statement is evidently meant to convey the impression that the religion of the Hawaiians exists on the surface, and on the surface only ; that it has no place in the hearts of the people, no hold on their affections, and that therefore it was necessary to send them a different kind of Christianity. Of the religion of the great body of the Christians in Hawaii, the committee themselves were incapable of forming a reliable opinion, but in relation to individuals of that people, they had evidence which should have prevented their spreading over the dioceses of England, a statement calculated to produce such injurious impressions without the clearest evidence of their truth.

Queen Emma herself was a Christian before the new missionaries set foot in Hawaii. Her Majesty's Chaplain was a Christian, was baptized, was received to the Communion of the Hawaiian Church, and continued

---

* "Hawaiian Church Mission." pp. 2, 3.

in " full standing " in that Church before he ever saw a Reformed Catholic missionary. Is their's, it may be asked, only a surface religion? Do the promoters of the new Mission deem it such? On the contrary, the extent to which they have associated them with their public religious services here warrants the inference that they regard them as genuine Christians.

As a few ears of corn are a sample of the sheaves of the field from which they are taken, so these acknowledged Christians are living witnesses that the Christianity of the Sandwich Islanders is not a mere surface covering, veiling over a heathen belief and heathen practices, but the deeply rooted religion of the heart; and that the seed which the Hawaiian missionaries have sown in their hearts is the good seed of the Kingdom. And if, to continue the illustration, the field has long lain waste, filled with roots of rank and noxious weeds which, springing up, choke the good seed so that it should occasionally produce abortive growths, this would be no evidence that all were such, or that notwithstanding some disappointment there might not still be a harvest that should gladden the laborer's heart, and that should be gathered in at the last great harvest day.

I dismiss, however, the appeal of the committee with the single remark that it is much to be regretted that a body of Christian gentlemen, associated for the spread of the Gospel, should have felt themselves called upon to print and circulate a statement so calculated to injure a number of faithful laborers in that same work without being sure that it was true. There was no necessity for them to go out of their way to endeavor to condemn the work of the American missionaries and to show that they had been unfaithful to their trust. If they sought to obtain aid to carry on what they deemed their own work, it was enough to say, if they thought such was the fact, that there was a large portion of the people not brought under either Catholic or Protestant instruction.

Neither the King of the Sandwich Islands, nor the members of the Church of England there, when they applied for a clergyman, said anything about " a superficial Christianity thinly veiling a heathen faith and heathen practices." This, it would seem, like the want of a Bishop, remained to be discovered in England.

Still greater injustice is done to the American teachers by the declaration that the moral corruption of the heathen, aggravated by intercourse with foreigners, had become more rank under the religious system of the missionaries. Such a revolting charge shocks the sense of justice in all upright minds and carries with it its own condemnation.

That a writer in a religious periodical, devoted to the furtherance of religion in connection with the Church of England, and intended to be read by Christian men, should tell his readers that, as a matter of history, the American missionaries " made hypocrites as fast as they made proselytes," and farther, that the " moral corruption of the natives, aggravated by foreigners, became more rank under their religious system," are statements so utterly at variance with every credible account of their labors, that it must be doubted whether the writer believed them himself.

Since the year 1823, when the first convert was baptized, nearly 53,000 converts* have been received into the Hawaiian churches. To assert that more than 1,000 false professors of Christianity have every year, for more than forty years, been publicly baptized, and received to full standing in a Protestant Church, the charge against which is that its discipline is too strict and severe, is what few, if any, reflecting men will find themselves able to regard in any other light than as an unauthorized assertion, calculated to injure, in the opinion of others, an exemplary and faithful body of men. But to suppose, as any belief in these statements requires us to do, that the whole body of missionaries in the Sandwich Islands, to whom the reports of accessions to each church, or each district, were annually submitted, should deceive each other and the native brethren, or should unite to deceive the foreign residents in the Islands where these reports were published, exceeds all ordinary capacity of faith to such an extent that few will believe it can be true.

It seems also impossible for reflecting men to attach any credit to the assertion that the missionaries made hypocrites as fast as they made proselytes, because that would require us to believe that during these forty years, in which as great and beneficial a change as had taken place among any heathen people in the world had occurred, there had not been among the fifty thousand proselytes one sincere Christian. Not one soul there, whatever its repentance or faith, or holiness, or love and trust in Christ, and peace and hope in passing to the grave—not one that should be saved.

---

* Dr. Anderson's "Hawaiian Islands," p. 300.

The Roman Catholic Church teaches that outside the pale of that Church none can be saved, but no church that I have heard of teaches that hypocrites shall be saved, and, as a necessary consequence, we are required to believe that not one of these fifty thousand proselytes could be saved. This, it is true, appeared to be the opinion of one of the speakers at Chelmsford. The new Mission, he said, "Wanted more money, and more men;" and, in allusion to objections said, the first was "Why waste your energies and money on seventy thousand people, and they ten thousand miles away?" He is reported to have asked, "Did these people dare to tell him that these seventy thousand souls were unworthy of any effort?" and to have closed the sentence with the exclamation already quoted, "Good heavens! seventy thousand immortal souls not to be saved!"

Mournful indeed, and without a parallel in Christian missions, would be the result of forty years of faithful labor if this were true. Happily, for the encouragement of the friends of missions, the reverse is the case. The deaths of communicants in full standing during the forty years ending 1863, were 20,017,* and thousands of these had confessed a good confession, had borne in their lives what the Scripture calls the fruit of the Spirit,† and had experienced such a calm confiding close of a holy life as to warrant in survivors the hope that the departed had entered into blessedness and rest. And there are many still living, who, amidst much that is feeble in principle and defective in practice, and though some at times may be overcome by temptation, are yet striving to regulate their lives by God's Word, to experience more of the love of Christ in their hearts, and to grow in meetness for heaven. Among these, and connected with the American Mission Churches, Kekuanaoa, father of the King and step-father to Queen Emma, Kanoa, Governor of Kauai, and John Ii, one of the Judges of the Supreme Court, are living witnesses that the imputation cast on the proselytes of the American missionaries is unfounded.

It is said that the missionaries themselves confessed that the religion of the people was "little more than a name." On this it may be sufficient to observe that the missionaries never stated any such thing, but always the reverse. They represented their converts as in the infancy

---

* Dr. Anderson's "Hawaiian Islands," p. 300.
† Gal. i. 22, 23.

of their moral and religious life, manifesting all the feebleness and immaturity of such a state, that every onward step was resisted by the older and stronger principles of evil within them, in striving against which they often failed; but that, notwithstanding this fearful disadvantage, there had always been a goodly number who, they had reason to believe, though weak, were yet sincere.

The missionaries confessed that all were not sincere; that there were always some at times, and for a season many, whose religion seemed little more than a name, and that when such fell into sin they were excluded from the fellowship of the church, but pitied, wept over, pleaded with, and prayed for, that they might repent, forsake sin, and be restored. This was the sorrow of the missionary's heart—his cry in deep humiliation before God. It was no pleasure to him to publish it to the world. It was not to accuse another when he did so, but faithfully to report the progress of his own work, to excite the sympathy of others in his trials, and to call forth their prayers for himself and for the weak and erring members of his flock. These faithful reports of defects among the objects of his care ought not to be wrested to his disadvantage, but rather mentioned to his honor, and regarded as evidences of his trustworthiness.

And, after all, what do the defections amount to? The evidence adduced by those who condemn the Mission, shows that those who have disgraced their Christian character form, considering the general state of society, but a small proportion of the communicants. During forty years the whole number excommunicated were about 8,000, or less than one in seven of the entire body of church members.

The people have but recently emerged from a state of society in which virtue found no place, where vice was honored in proportion as it was unscrupulous, revolting, and destructive, and it had become, by length of time, ingrained into their very nature. The newly imbibed faith was still weak; Christian principle immature, and the requirements of the new religion imperfectly understood. Temptations were constant and common, and their danger neither clearly seen nor adequately felt amongst them, as compared with the members of older Christian communities; and, according to the most unquestionable evidence which can be adduced, there have been only 8,000 out of more than 50,000 Hawaiian converts who had, in the course of forty years, deviated so far from the required rectitude of conduct as to be, by the severe and strict discipline of the missionaries, excluded from the church.

There are conditions under which the aspect of religious life differs, and seasons in which its manifestations vary in kind and degree; but the figures above given include the seasons of greatest decline, as well as those of steadfastness, during forty years. With this evidence before us, we are constrained to believe that notwithstanding all just drawbacks, the American Mission in Hawaii is no failure, but may worthily rank with the most prosperous of modern missions.

There are yet two other impeachments of this Mission preferred by high dignitaries of the Church of England, which, from their gravity, as well as from the dignity and sacredness of the position of those who bring them forward, cannot be overlooked. The Bishop of Oxford, if the reporters for the public journals be correct,[*] stated at Salisbury, "The people are craving for your teachers; they are wearied out by the mismanagement of the American Puritans." And in another place, his lordship is reported to have said that the missionaries "had created against themselves the strongest possible prejudice in this way."

Had there been this extreme prejudice against the American missionaries, this weariness of their mismanagement, this craving for the Reformed Catholic missionaries, it was naturally to be supposed that the former would have been forsaken. And if, as another advocate of this Mission affirms, "it was the religion of England, to be brought from England by the long promised teachers that all along fed the national expectation;" if the "Hawaiians were looking with an eager eye to the church of the future;" if "the Ark of God was still due across the waters;" and if "all that was required was to see teachers appear," and "to whom all were prepared to listen;"[†] if these things were so, it is natural to suppose that when tidings of the arrival of this ardently desired boon, which had "all along fed the national expectation," were made known, the heart of Hawaii, throughout all its coasts, would have beat with unwonted pleasure, and that the the "craving" throngs from Puna to Kauai would have hurried to Honolulu to welcome and to look upon the men by whom their "craving" was to be appeased; and that as all that was required was to see these teachers, "to whom all were

---

[*] "Daily News." October 26th, 1865.
[†] "Colonial Church Chronicle," p. 352.

prepared to listen,"* that no place of worship would have contained the multitude that would have crowded together to hear their preaching.

Some such manifestation of popular feeling would have been reasonable if the above statements made to show the necessity for the recently sent Mission ever had any foundation. The Mission was inaugurated on the day of a great national festival by a splendid ceremonial, when the late King and his Queen were confirmed. The people had also been favored with the opportunity of attending the ministrations of the Bishop and his assistants, and of seeing the accompaniments of their worship. And yet it appears, on the authority of a work on missions, compiled by a clergyman of the Church of England, and published last year, that the number of communicants in connection with the Reformed Catholic Mission was, in 1864, one hundred, and of attendants on the ministry of Bishop Staley and that of his three presbyters, seven hundred and fifty.†

But at Wiston the most remarkable description of the people, and of the doctrine and practice of the missionaries, was given. The Bishop of Oxford is reported to have said :—" These children of nature, children of the air, children of the light, children of the sun, children of beauty, disporting themselves for the most part in the open air, living in the utmost conceivable freedom, taking their greatest pleasure in the dance, dancing many times a day, dancing almost every evening, and then imagine these people visited by the descendants of the stern old Puritans of New England, if anything, rather more severe, sour, and vinegar-like, carrying with them the iron code of Connecticut, the most severe ever inflicted upon any people on the earth, taking peculiar examples from the Levitical law, and applying them to Christian times, by a strange mistake, which pervaded the old Puritan mind, that Christianity found its excellence by a retrogression to Judaism. For instance, they wrote it down in their code that if any father had a troublesome child he should bring him before the elders, and he should be stoned. These men, many of them good men, very devout men, men who really desired the salvation of the souls of these poor islanders, and came for that purpose and no other, who gave up their homes that they might come, but coming with all the bias and severity of Puritan life to these children of nature, these children of the sun. And then conceive the moral and social ef-

---

* "Colonial Church Chronicle," p. 352.
† "Missionary Geography."

fervescence that ensued. They were commanded not to put away sensuality merely, but all that was child-like, spiritual and unobjectionable in their habits, removing the eternal landmarks between morality and immorality, teaching them that things innocent, like things wicked, were to be condemned. Here was a great mistake, arising out of the injured form of Christianity which they were desiring to inculcate."

At Leeds his lordship is reported in the same journal* to have said, " The American missionaries preached not what we believed to be the completeness of the Christian system, and there were many peculiarities about their teaching which were most distinctly hostile to all the natural tendencies of that peculiar people—a people given to gaiety, endowed with a sort of perpetual youth, and not capable of enduring the severity with which, from the most conscientious convictions, their new teachers came among them. The consequence is, that from this and other causes, they have not got hold of the hearts of the people."

These remarkable passages do not require notice, except on account of their having been employed in justification of the Reformed Catholic Mission, and for this purpose they do not seem to be very appropriate. They describe the Sandwich Islanders as among the most highly favored of the human family—" Children of the light, children of the sun, children of beauty," and as taking " their greatest pleasure in the dance, dancing continually," a people of gaiety, endowed with a sort of perpetual youth. Such a people would seem to have escaped the calamity of the Fall; they could scarcely need the teaching of any Mission, and must have approached nearly to the paradisaical condition of mankind.

I have visited, resided, and traveled in this country. I have mingled with these people in the public, social and religious engagements of life, and neither I nor my companions found them as here described. Their personal appearance and condition are greatly improved, and so are their dress, their dwellings, and their habits of social life, since my residence amongst them, which was the period referred to, viz: when the Puritan missionaries first went to the Islands. At that period, the high chiefs and some of the middle class exhibited fine and noble forms of symmetry and strength, and at times wore good and decent clothing, yet at times. even among the very highest, the clothing was nothing more for the men than a girdle a few inches wide, and for the women a piece of cloth

---

* " Daily News."

wrapped round the waist and reaching a little below the knees. The dwellings, especially of the lower classes, were low dark huts, chiefly of grass. Their filthiness was disgusting, such as scarcely admits of description; and this, added to many loathsome diseases, rendered many of them the most pitiable, yet at the same time, the most sickening and revolting objects which the eye could behold. In this respect they were below the Society Islanders, probably because their country was colder, their means of living less abundant, and the streams of fresh water for bathing, comparatively few.

Nothing but a feeling of compassion, as Mr. Stewart observed, "sometimes bordering on agony," a desire to make an effort to induce these people to rise, a belief that they, low as they were, were immortal, and that God's grace was sufficient for their entire regeneration, could have taken us a second time to their abodes, and to the companionship of such debasement and wretchedness. These feelings were shared by us all. Dr. Stewart, who was stationed on the island called Maui, in his published journal, referring to an evening walk along the beach, observes:—" The largest hut I passed was not higher than my waist; capable only of containing a family, like pigs in a sty, on a bed of dried grass, filled with vermin. Not a bush or shrub was to be seen around, or any appearance whatever of cultivation. It was the time of their evening repast, and most of the people were seated on the ground eating *poi*, surrounded by swarms of flies, and sharing their food with dogs, pigs and ducks, who helped themselves freely from the dishes of their masters." And again : " There are not a few of the manners and habits of the people that can never be mentioned, but which daily and hourly obtrude themselves on the observation." These and other causes of disgust and repulsion were then so common, " as to be without reproach, except in the eyes of a foreigner." The same writer, speaking of fearful diseases prevailing amongst the people, states that they " annually consign hundreds to the grave, and convert others, while living, into walking sepulchres."

This devoted missionary, a man of refined mind and habits, who had left a position of respect and comfort, thus gives vent to his feelings in connection with his work :—" Notwithstanding the abominations daily taking place around us, drunkenness, adultery, gambling, and theft, deceit, treachery, and violence, all of which exist throughout the land to an almost incredible degree, such has already been the success attending the efforts at reformation, made in the very infancy of the Mission, that we are encouraged, by every day's observance, with fresh zeal to dedicate ourselves to the work of rescue and salvation. They are still uncivilized heathens, living, not only in all the simplicity, but in all the vulgarity of untutored nature :—and I can sincerely say, that in them I see much that I love, and more that I admire,—I must in candor add— and much, if not all, that I abhor." Sodom and Gomorrah were scarcely more vile.

How far the condition of the Sandwich Islanders, nearly fifty years ago, when the Puritans first arrived in the country, resembled the mental picture of these people, which the Bishop of Oxford sketched with such exuberance of metaphor at Wiston and at Leeds, designating them "children of the air," and a "people of gaiety, endowed with perpetual youth," the readers of the foregoing description of these same people as they were, by personal intercourse, found to be, must decide for themselves.

That portion of the eulogium on this people devoted to their dances, occasions me extreme regret that his lordship did not make himself better acquainted with the character and practices associated with their heathen dances, for if he had done so I cannot believe that he would ever have given the slightest sanction, much less even implied, commendation of practices which, if not always, were generally, and almost inevitably, occasions of the most disgraceful and revolting wickedness.

Evidence of the true character of these dances was not far to seek. Few readers of the narratives of our early voyagers can be ignorant of the fact that although at times there may have been nothing opposed to decency, these dances were incentives to vice as well as occasions for its indulgence. Vancouver, an authority often quoted by the promoters of the new Mission, describing one of these dances, observes : "Had the performance finished with the third act, we should have retired from their theatre with a much higher idea of the moral tendency of their drama than was conveyed by the offensive scene exhibited by the ladies in the concluding part. The language of the song no doubt corresponded with the display which was carried to a degree of extravagance calculated to produce nothing but disgust even to the most licentious."[*]

[*] Vancouver. vol. iii., p. 45.

Mr. Stewart, in describing the effect on his own mind of these dances taking place near to where he was, states that " the sounds of their rude music, the wild notes of their songs, reached us even in the Mission enclosure. But they fell on the heart with a saddening power, for we had been compelled already, from our own observation, as well as from the communications of others, necessarily to associate with them exhibitions of unrivalled licentiousness, and abominations which must forever remain untold. I can never forget the impressions made upon my mind the first few nights after coming to anchor in the harbor, while these songs and dances were in preparation by rehearsal and practice. With the gathering darkness of every evening, thousands of the natives assembled in a grove of cocoanut trees near the ship; and the fires round which they danced were scarcely ever extinguished till the break of day, while the shouts of revelry and licentiousness, shouts of which till then I had no conception, and which are heard only in a heathen land, unceasingly burst upon the ear."

I once, when residing at Honolulu, went in obedience to a message from the Queen to a place where, to my surprise and disgust, a sort of rehearsal of one of these dances was going on; and almost before I was fully aware of what it was, the filthy picture seemed to be burned as with vitriol into my mind as I turned and hurried home from the spot.

Such were the chief part of the dances which, if the Bishop of Oxford's description of the Sandwich Islands be correct, formed their "chief occupation and their greatest pleasure." Happily for the people it is not correct, for had they danced many times in the day, and almost every evening, it must have greatly accelerated the already rapid diminution of their numbers. There were some who danced for their bread, as dancers do with us, and not for pleasure. The common people seldom danced among themselves, or for their own amusement, generally for that of their chiefs, or the visitors of their chiefs, and at great festivals. On these occasions, with very rare, if any exceptions, the dances were practiced as stimulants to vice, or occasions for its practice. Few dances took place in the day, they were generally practiced in the evening, or under cover of the night. To call these innocent dances is to shock all sense of decency and virtue, and can scarcely be imagined as arising from anything but the most unaccountable delusion.

For the suppression of these dances the missionaries and their creed are severely censured. Such censure every right-minded man and woman throughout Christendom, who knows anything about the matter, will consider most erroneously placed, and will probably deem the missionaries, if they did suppress them, entitled to the highest praise. It is, however, doubtful whether it was necessary for the missionaries to take any steps towards this end. So long as the chiefs and people disregarded the religious teachings of the missionaries, the protests of the latter against this source of wickedness, or against drunkenness, or any other vices which drown men's souls in perdition, would have been utterly disregarded. But when once the pure and holy doctrines of the Gospel entered the hearts of the natives, their knowledge of the power of these dances to excite the grossest passions, and that they were intended and expected to issue in vice, would prevent their thinking for a moment that the indwelling of religion in the heart, and countenance of these dances, much less participation in them, could be deemed compatible. They would themselves prohibit them as much as they would prohibit idol worship, and would no more think of joining in such obscene proceedings than of offering human sacrifices.

The revival of these heathen dances, for it is these alone, if any, that the Puritans have suppressed, would outrage the Christian feeling of the better portion of the community, native and foreign.* Yet it is the cessation of these that is so mournfully deplored. Dancing of a respectable kind is not suppressed. A writer in an American commercial and merchants' magazine for 1858, speaks of the evening polka *reunions* at Honolulu, in which natives and foreigners united; and a gentleman, the son of a physician, a near neighbor of mine, an officer in the navy, who, a few years ago, was at home for awhile, when he found that I had been at Hawaii, spoke sometimes of the pleasant evenings he had spent at Honolulu, where he had waltzed with Queen Emma, and seemed to have enjoyed the respectable and agreeable society which he had met with there.

Other assertions said to have been made at Wiston, I may, perhaps, allude to before I close; but I could not allow the suppression of the intentionally demoralizing heathen dances to be adduced as a ground of

---

* A few years ago the foreigners opened a theatre at Honolulu. The natives said it was a kind of *hula* dancing, and revived some of their own, to the grief of the respectable portion of the community. The Governor would not allow them anywhere but at Honolulu, and they have since, I believe, been discontinued.

censure either of the missionaries or their teaching without an earnest protest.

The Bishop of Honolulu, who also laments the discontinuance of the former dances, surpasses all others in the startling and paradoxical accusations which he brings against the deeply injured missionaries. I select only two of these. In a pastoral address, published in Honolulu at the beginning of the past year, Bishop Staley prefers the following monstrously extravagant charge against them : " There was less of fearful corruption in the heathen, than in the Christian days of the people. The change for the worse, I do not hesitate to say, has been greatly aided by Puritanism, working partly by faulty legislation, partly by the religious unreality which it too generally fosters."

In the number of " Evangelical Christendom " for January this year, there is an account of a visit paid by Bishop Staley to America ; and in his appeal for men and money to assist in the work, he is stated to have said, that under the influence of the existing Christianity the morals of the people are to day " ten times worse than they were under the heathen system," that their piety is an " unctuous cant," and that the professors of this Christianity are relapsing into " heathenism, sorcery, and witchcraft." And he quotes in proof an expression of the missionaries which applies to a particular locality, as though it applied to a large community. All these evils, the writer adds, are described, not as the result of a conflict which human depravity and long continued national vices, aggravated by the worst sort of imported temptations, are waging against Christianity itself, but as the *natural fruit of the Congregational and Presbyterian Churches* of New York and Philadelphia, of New England and of all in the United States, who constitute the American Board. Upon this plea, Bishop Staley presented himself before the House of Bishops of the Episcopal Church of this country.*

It may suffice in adverting to these depreciatory statements to remark that their author cannot be a competent witness as to what corruption prevailed at Hawaii in the days of heathenism ; nor is he much better qualified to testify to the moral state of the people generally at the present time. His testimony must be based on the statements of others; and when he uttered the extravagant assertion that there was less corruption among the people when they were heathen than at the present

---

* " Evangelical Christendom," January, 1866. p. 31.

time, and added, "The change for the worse, I do not hesitate to say, has been greatly aided by Puritanism, * * * and partly by the religious unreality which it too generally fosters," he uttered assertions which were as unfounded as they are uncharitable.

The assertion that the moral corruption of the people is worse—"ten times worse"—since they have become Christians than while they were heathen, can only be substantiated by witnesses acquainted with the heathen as well as with the Christian state of the people, and these witnesses bear a directly opposite testimony. It is sufficient at present to adduce the evidence of the missionaries, some of whom arrived there before there was a single native Christian in the Islands, and have lived among the people for nearly fifty years. These men have borne their testimony publicly face to face with their accusers, before authorities from their own country; and their testimony, which has received the highest confirmation, is directly contrary to the accusations preferred against them.

Charges of the baneful effects of their management and teaching had been made, not by the natives but by foreigners, in the year 1827.

Some months afterwards, a captain of the United States Navy arrived at the Islands. The missionaries demanded a public investigation. In the statement of their proceedings, after alluding to the effects of their labors in diminishing drunkenness, gambling, &c., they proceed to say, "While we allude to these charges, we are far from being blind or indifferent to the barbarism, fickleness, duplicity, neglect, laziness, and other varied vices and crimes, which to some extent still remain, and which are more or less visible even to a transient visitor; neither do we vindicate, or in the least degree offer a palliation for these things. We only complain and remonstrate against those illiberal and unmanly charges by which the Mission is made accountable for the daily blunders, the childish actions, the long-established customs, and even the inherent depravity of the people; and all, forsooth, because we attempt to make them better.

"If the doctrines and duties of Christianity, in which the Church of England, the Church of Scotland, the Presbyterian, and other churches in America are agreed, are not adapted to correct the evils which exist in heathen nations; have no good influence to cure the evils of the human heart, and to promote virtue, order, and happiness in society, then we may challenge the wisdom of the world to devise a system of morals, and to propose any practicable measures, which will raise a savage tribe or a heathen nation from their native depravity to a state of civilization and virtuous life.

"If then we have mistaken the grand principles of reformation, or if we have taken a wrong step, we will be grateful to any man who, in a friendly manner, will inform us of it. *If we have spoken or done evil, bear witness of the evil; but if well, why should we be smitten?*

"From those gentlemen who reside, or occasionally touch at these Islands, we ask an investigation of our conduct. We do more—we challenge it.

"We have here stated our whole object, and also the means we use to obtain it. We know that the cold-hearted, the misanthropical, and the superstitious heathen, will be opposed to the former, and will charge all the crimes and defects which still remain to the latter. But there are those around us, and those who occasionally visit us from abroad, who can judge candidly. We request them to examine the above statements, and we on our part pledge ourselves that if we may have a candid hearing, with witnesses, we will substantiate everything which we here assert."

In due course a public meeting for investigation took place at the house of the brother of the Regent, before Captain Jones of the United States Navy, and a number of his officers. The missionaries and their accusers were there, and the former engaged to reply to any accusation preferred in writing against them.

What was the result? No charge was brought forward; no evidence against the missionaries was adduced, although their calumniators sustained, according to the account of Captain Jones, "the fourfold relation of prosecutor, witness, jury, and judge! And yet," asks Captain Jones, in his published account of this meeting,[*] "what was the issue of this great trial? *The most perfect, full, complete and triumphant victory* for the missionaries that could have been asked by their most devoted friends. Not one *jot* or *tittle*, not one *iota* derogatory to their character as *men*, or as ministers of the Gospel of the strictest order, or

---

[*] Jarves' "History," p. 271. quoted in "Lectures on the Past and Present of the Sandwich Islands, by T. Dwight Hunt, pastor," and published in San Francisco, 1853.

as missionaries, could be made to appear *by the united efforts of all* who conspired against them."

To this testimony may be added that of the venerable chief, Kekuanaoa, father of the late and present King, and for many years past a blameless Christian. It was delivered in the large stone church in Honolulu, on a public occasion in 1841, and was published at the time. "In looking," says the Governor, "over the years that are past, I see great reason to praise God for His goodness to me, and to all who are here present. I look back to the reign of Kamehameha I., and around on the present state of things, and I say there is no being so great and so good as Jehovah, and there are no laws so good as his." * * * "Uncleanness abounded in our times of darkness. Some chief men had ten wives: some had more, and some had less. So also those who had property had many women. Neither were the women confined each to one man. The law of marriage was then unknown. Untold evils arose from this source, such as infanticide, quarrels, murder, and such like things. All these evils are not done away, but they have greatly decreased." * * * "We are better clad than we used to be. I remember the time when we saw only the *kika* and the *malo* (girdle) among the common people. Great, indeed, was the thieving in our days of ignorance. It was connected with lying and robbery in every quarter. Laziness was thought to be honorable; and lazy people were the greatest favorites with the chiefs. When a chief died, there were dreadful doings. Teeth were knocked out; uncleanness was seen everywhere in open day; food was destroyed, and every sort of abomination was committed.

"I will now speak of Liholiho's reign. He made a law, called *makahonu*, on the death of his father. Great was our rum-drinking, dancing, singing, stealing, adultery and night-carousing at that time. Whole nights were spent in debauchery. Very good were all these things to my mind in those days. But latterly I have become acquainted with the Word of God, and the Law of God, showing a better way than any I knew before. Let us bless the name of Jehovah for all his benefits to us and our nation. Blessed is the man who keeps the law of the Lord."

In a letter from the young King, at an earlier period, viz., in 1836, he had said—"Love to you, our obliging friends in America. This is our sentiment as to promoting the order and prosperity of these Hawaiian

Islands. Give us additional teachers, like the teachers who dwell in your own country."*

In 1848, the "entire body of missionaries, then numbering twenty-nine clergymen, all of them liberally educated, and twelve intelligent laymen, bore a united testimony to the favorable contrast between the state of the people at that time, as compared with their state at the commencement of the Mission." I bring down the evidence of these competent witnesses to 1863, as it is given by Dr. Anderson, who says, "I heard all the missionary brethren had to say on the subject during the four months that I remained in the Islands, and I feel assured that multitudes of those whom I had the happiness to address, and take by the hand, how low soever they may stand on the scale of intelligence and social life, are to be numbered with the people of God." * * * "As compared with *their own past*—which is the proper comparison—they have been greatly elevated." * * * " They were then naked barbarians. Lying, drunkenness, theft, robbery, were universal. So was licentiousness, and it was shameless in open day. There was no restraint on polygamy and polyandry. Mothers buried their infant children alive, and children did the same with their aged and infirm parents." * * * " I did not see a drunken native while on the Islands. Theft and robbery are less frequent there than in the United States. We slept at night with open doors, had no apprehension, and lost nothing. Licentiousness still largely exists outside the church, and is one of the easily-besetting sins within it; but it now everywhere shuns the day, and is subjected to the discipline of the church. Nor do mothers any more bury their infant children alive, nor children their aged and infirm parents."†

To this long line of evidence, which I believe to be irrefragable, I add one additional testimony, of greater weight in reference to the condition of the people in the days of heathenism, and equally strong and clear in favor of the teaching of the missionaries. It was given at the time when an Englishman wearing, but disgracing by his conduct, the uniform of our own country, united with a number of others in urging the expulsion of the missionaries, on the ground that their teaching and influence was fast plunging the country into civil war and bloodshed. The witness to whom I now refer, whose loyalty to this country through

* Dr. Anderson. p. 76. † Ibid, p. 289.

forty years of absence never failed, who had been the most trusted adviser of the first Kamehameha, and for nine years Governor of Hawaii; who was the grandfather of Queen Emma, and until his death exercised a wise and beneficial influence over the counsels of the Government, bore the following straightforward English testimony :—

"Whereas, it has been represented by many persons, that the labors of the missionaries in these Islands are attended with evil and disadvantage to the people, I hereby most cheerfully give my testimony to the contrary. I am fully convinced that the good which is accomplishing, and already effected, is not little. The great and radical change already made for the better, in the manners and customs of this people, has far surpassed my most sanguine expectations. During the forty years that I have resided here, I have known thousands of defenseless human beings cruelly massacred in their exterminating wars. I have seen multitudes of my fellow-beings offered in sacrifice to their idol gods. I have seen this large island, once filled with inhabitants, dwindle down to its present numbers through wars and disease, and I am persuaded that nothing but Christianity can preserve them from total extinction. I rejoice that true religion is taking the place of superstition and idolatry, that good morals are superseding the reign of crime, and that a code of Christian laws is about to take the place of tyranny and oppression. These things are what I have long wished for, but have never seen till now. I thank God that in my old age I see them, and humbly trust I feel them too."*

The above testimony was given at the close of 1826, by Mr. John Young. It is not even hinted that the teaching or the management of the missionaries has changed since then. Their own testimony declares that the morals of the people are better, perhaps inconceivably so to those who have no personal acquaintance with the deep corruption of unmitigated heathenism ; and it will require something more than the carefully worded affirmation of the Committee of the Reformed Catholic Mission, that a "surface Christianity thinly veils heathen belief and heathen practices ; " the fascinating but unreal delineation of the former condition of the people; or the "I hesitate not to say, that the morals of the people are to day ten times worse than they were under the heathen system," of Bishop Staley to invalidate this testimony. With

* Dr. Anderson, p. 67.

the above evidence before them, the great body of the friends of Protestant missions in Europe and America, will not believe that the teaching of the American missionaries is so defective, and their management so disastrous, as to require, or even to justify the attempt to draw away the people from the teaching of the Americans to that of the Reformed Catholic Bishop and his missionaries.

The terms by which Bishop Staley designates the religion of the Islanders I decline to repeat or notice. He speaks of the faulty legislation introduced by the missionaries; and the accusation is repeated elsewhere more than once. It is said, " they made the grave mistake of introducing themselves into the secular offices of the Kingdom, to such an extent that some of the leading men among them who had originally come there in a missionary character, afterwards dropped that character, merged into political intriguers, and took purely secular callings, promoting their aggrandizement, instead of the Kingdom of Christ."*

Accusations, such as these, do not come very well from parties who, if such conduct be culpable, have been themselves much more so. It was long before any missionary could be induced to render that aid which the Government had vainly sought elsewhere; but the Bishop of Honolulu, one of the accusers of the missionaries, had been in the country but a very short time before he became a member of the King's Privy Council, and has since, it is said, been made a member of the Board of Public Education, though still remaining at the head of his Mission. The Americans ceased to be connected with their Mission before they engaged in any business of the Government.†

The first instance of this kind which occurred was that of Mr. Richards. The destruction of the tabu had swept away the foundation of their former Government; the adoption of Christianity rendered Government necessary. The rulers wished to assimilate, as far as possible, their proceedings to that of civilized and Christian nations. In these circumstances, they turned their eyes towards their teachers for assistance. But, in accordance with an established rule, the latter declined to act, otherwise than as they had always done, *to give advice when asked.* The kingdom they had come to establish was not of this world. They therefore referred the Government to the United States for help.

---

* "Colonial Church Chronicle" for September, 1865.
† Dwight Hunt's Lectures, p. 143.

Accordingly, in 1835, the King and chiefs wrote to the Board of Missions at Boston to obtain a suitable person to become counsellor and teacher of political economy to the Government. The Board made every effort for this purpose but failed.* On hearing of this the chiefs renewed their application to the Mission.

About this time Mr. Richards, a missionary high in the esteem and confidence of the nation, after fourteen years' faithful labor, returned from the United States, whither he had gone to provide for the education of his children, and was invited on his arrival to become political counsellor and teacher to the King and chiefs. He had returned to live and die a humble pastor of the native church which he had gathered during former years, * * * and he naturally shrunk from the task, but on the recommendation of his brethren and the American Board,† he accepted the King's offer, and entered on his duties in 1838,‡ three years after the first application had been made, and for so doing the Mission is censured and held up to ridicule.

In respect to their relations to Government, the nature of the teaching of the missionaries was distinctly set forth in a series of resolutions, adopted June, 1838—which the late Mr. Wyllie, Minister of Foreign Affairs, pronounced "worthy to be printed in letters of gold, and hung up in the House of Nobles." He also said, "The assertion sometimes made that 'the missionaries, individually, wormed themselves into the confidence of the King and chiefs, in order to exercise an influence favorable to themselves and to the United States,' is a bold and unscrupulous assertion, without even a shadow of truth."§

I have now endeavored to test the validity of some of the specific accusations against the American missionaries, which are assigned as reasons for commencing and continuing the new Mission. But these reasons are as remarkable for their omissions, as for what they include.

That a nation which, little more than forty years ago, was as ignorant

---

* Dwight Hunt's Lectures. p. 143. † Ibid, p. 145.
‡ In 1843 the Islands had been outrageously seized by an English officer. After their restoration to the King by Admiral Thomas, Mr. Richards, in company with a native chief, was sent to England to arrange for the future security of the Islands. He was received with courtesy and treated with respect by the Earl of Aberdeen, and succeeded so far as to secure a convention between the Governments of England and France, mutually guaranteeing the independence of the Sandwich Islands. I had the pleasure of renewing intercourse with my friend both in London and in Paris. At his death, the Government voted a pension to his widow, which was regularly paid so long as she lived.
§ Dr. Anderson, p. 84.

and almost as savage as the kingdom of Dahomy, should now have their common day schools spread over the whole surface of the country, giving on an average, during a large portion of that time, a good plain education to one-sixth of the population; having, besides these, their high schools, and their college, is perhaps, next to the acceptance of Christianity, the most conclusive evidence of improvement that any nation can give. This work, in all its gradations from the alphabet upwards, the American missionaries have accomplished. They have succeeded in a manner which, as I shall presently show, has called forth, from thoroughly competent witnesses, the highest commendation; and yet in all the accounts which I have seen of the condition of the people among whom it is proposed to place this new Mission, only the slightest mention is made of this truly great achievement of the American teachers, and that generally accompanied with disparaging statements.

Even Bishop Staley, when enumerating the perfectly marvellous scholastic attainments of the late amiable and truly excellent King, who at the age of twenty-one succeeded to the throne, after repeating his Majesty's remark, in reference to the translation of the Bible, that the missionaries had "in their ignorance of Hebrew made sad mistakes," appears to have taken it for granted that the King was perfectly competent to pronounce upon the missionaries' knowledge or ignorance of Hebrew; and proceeds to state, without any allusion to the uncommon teaching which the King must have received, that he could enjoy "Kingsley, Thackeray, Tennyson, and was ever quoting Shakespeare, but that the habit of his mind was still theological." That he "loved to dwell on the regularity of the English orders, and few laymen could vindicate, with the same ability, every link in the chain of their transmission;" and his lordship adds, "He was familiar with the works of Wheatley, Palmer, Courayer, Percival," &c.; "he used to remark on the soundness of our position as a church; that of Scripture 'interpreted by the old fathers;' for, he used to say, the waters become purer as you approach the fountain."

I make no remark upon this wonderful account, and notice it only to express my regret that no word of commendation is bestowed upon the teachers of the King, for his Majesty had none besides these same "stern, sour, vinegar-like, narrow-minded, uneducated Puritans."

Any tutor or tutors in another land, whose industry and talent should have implanted in a royal pupil such ability to enjoy polite literature, and yet extend his studies to such generally unattractive subjects as Hebrew criticism, the writings of the old fathers, and the tracing of every link in the chain of the transmission of the orders in the English Church, would have been, it might naturally be supposed, entitled to the high estimation of all members of that church; or, at least, to respect and encouragement, if not to something more substantial, instead of being accused of having failed in their work, and having this accusation assigned as a reason for their being supplanted by their accusers.

There is, however, one thing which appears to me to be a discovery. Bishop Staley speaks of the young King as having "had the strong religious instincts of his race," and it is to be inferred that this instinct rendered "the habit of his mind theological." I have no recollection of having seen any strong religious instincts in the race, except in relation to their idolatry, nor of having heard such attributed to them by others; and if it be so, I can only say it is very remarkable. Bishop Staley, however, on this point, appears to have changed his opinion, for I find it stated in an American paper,* that in a document which his lordship put forth before leaving the Sandwich Islands, he said: "I am bound to record what is the result of my intercourse with the Hawaiians. They have anything but an intelligent acquaintance with Holy Scripture. Of its composite character—of the times and circumstances of the authors, when they wrote the various books, they know nothing. They do not in fact possess that historical and common information which can alone render its perusal profitable and even safe. No attempt seems to have been made to teach them how to distinguish the human from the divine, in the inspired volume; eternal principles from what is temporary and incidental."

The editor of the paper remarks: "We call attention to this extract, and claim that Bishop Colenso goes no further in his disbelief in a divinely inspired Bible, than Bishop Staley, and, without amplifying, ask a careful reading of the paragraph."

The only observation I offer, at present, on this testimony of Bishop Staley's, is, that I cannot perceive how this and the statement previously cited, can both be correct. If, as the Bishop states, religious instincts were not an idiosyncrasy of the late King, but "peculiar to his race,"

---

* The Boston "Congregationalist."

they must have been shared by the nation at large; and the intercourse of the Bishop with the Hawaiians, must have extended to the best educated among the inhabitants of Honolulu, including the Court, the members of which received the same teaching as the lamented Kamehameha IV. How is it, then, for they are all Hawaiians, that they do not possess along with their knowledge of the Holy Scriptures, that "historical and common information which can alone render their perusal profitable, and even safe?"

Besides the high attainments of the late King, there is other and unobjectionable testimony to the excellence of both the common and high schools in Hawaii. In relation to the former, the united body of missionaries, in 1865, publicly state:

"The schools have been carried on with the usual success and benefit to the Hawaiian youth. The instruction has, as in times past, been elementary in its character, nothing more. And this, under God, is our joy and our boast; not that we have founded and sustained a system for supplying a finished education for the more favored few, but a thoroughly sound and inestimably valuable elementary education for the masses of this nation. We deal with facts, not with pictures of the imagination; and in proof of the too little that we have heretofore cared to say in defense of the Hawaiian system of common schools, and the much more that might have been, and doubtless ought to have been said, to set forth its excellent adaptedness to the end proposed, we point, with unfeigned thankfulness to God, and with an honest pride, which we have no right to conceal, *to the nation as it stands before us to-day.* We exult in the thought that at this moment, a few of the most highly favored spots in New England excepted, not a nation exists on the face of the earth, so large a proportion of whose members are as well grounded in reading, writing, and common arithmetic."*

In 1860, Richard H. Dana, Esq., a distinguished lawyer, and a member of the Episcopal Church in Boston, United States, in a published narrative of his visit to the Sandwich Islands, gives the following testimony to the character of the Mission teaching:

"It is no small thing to say of the missionaries of the American Board, that in less than forty years they have taught this whole people to read and to write, to cipher and to sew. They have given them an

---

* "American Missionary Herald," November, 1865.

alphabet, grammar, and dictionary; preserved their language from extinction; given it a literature, and translated into it the Bible, and works of devotion, science, and entertainment, &c.

"In every district are free schools for natives. In these they are taught reading, writing, singing by note, arithmetic, grammar, and geography, by native teachers. At Lahainaluna is the Normal School for natives, where the best scholars from the district schools are received and carried to an advanced stage of education, and those who desire it are fitted for the duties of teachers. This was originally a Mission School, but is now partly a Government institution. Several of the missionaries, in small and remote stations, have schools for advanced studies, among which I visited several times that of Mr. Lyman, at Hilo, where there are nearly one hundred native lads; and all the under-teachers are natives. These lads had an orchestra of ten or twelve flutes, which made very creditable music. At Honolulu there is a royal school for natives, and another middle school for whites and half-castes; for it has been found expedient generally to separate the races in education. Both these schools are in excellent condition. But the special pride of the missionary efforts for education is the High School or College of Punahou. This was established for the education of the children of the Mission families, and has been enlarged to receive the children of other foreign residents, and is now an incorporated college, with some seventy scholars. The course of studies goes as far as the end of the Sophomore year in our New England colleges, and is expected soon to go farther. The teachers are young men of the Mission families, taught first at this school, with educations finished in the colleges of New England, where they have taken high rank. At Williams College there were at one time five pupils from this school, one of whom was the first scholar, and four of whom were among the first seven scholars of the year; and another of the professors at Punahou was the first scholar of his year at New Haven. I attended several recitations at Punahou in Greek, Latin, and mathematics; and after having said that the teachers were leading scholars in our colleges, and the pupils mostly children of the Mission families, I need hardly add that I advised the young men to remain there to the end of the course, as they could not pass the Freshman and Sophomore years more profitably elsewhere in my judgment. The examinations in Latin and Greek were particularly thorough in etymology and syntax. The Greek was read both by the quantity and by the printed accent, and the teachers were disposed to follow the Continental pronunciation of the vowels in the classic languages, if that system should be adopted in the New England colleges."

The external signs of improvement in dress, dwellings, and deportment, apparent among a large portion of the community, so unexpectedly pleasing to an intelligent visitor, who may remember the accounts of Cook, Vancouver, and other early voyagers, must be ascribed in part at least to the example, teaching and encouragement of the American missionaries.

The substitution for despotism and oppressive serfdom, of liberty, civil and religious, defined and guaranteed by solemn compact between the ruler and the people, is a benefit which, at least, the teachings of the missionaries must have predisposed the minds of rulers to give, and the people to receive. And although this great change has tended to restrain outrage and vice, has raised a shield over virtue, guaranteed security to person and property, encouraged enterprise, and favored commerce, as well as all that distinguishes a civilized from a savage people, these efforts have not received one word of commendation, and have only been mentioned to be ridiculed or condemned.

The foreign gentlemen engaged in commerce, cultivation, and other departments of honorable enterprise, of whom there have always been a number, the example of their families, and the influence of distinguished and friendly visitors to the Islands, have done much to promote the moral improvement and social progress of the people, as well as to strengthen the hands and often cheer the hearts of the missionaries. All honor to them for the stand they have taken on the side of purity, justice and right, and for the aid they have given to the cause of religion, civilization, and progress.

The history of the Hawaiian Mission abounds with instances of persons possessing a good acquaintance with Holy Scriptures, and giving evidence in spirit and in conduct of the work of the Holy Spirit, the influence of the grace of Christ, the word of Christ, and the love of Christ on their hearts through a long series of years. Kekuanaoa, the King's father, John Ii, Judge of the Supreme Court, who was a Christian when I was there, and is a Christian still, and who, with thousands of others, have given such satisfactory evidence through a large portion of their lives that their religion was a divinely implanted living principle, as to leave no doubt that they were sincere Christians. Yet I have seen no favorable notice of this fact, which has filled the hearts of many in Europe and America with grateful joy. The labors of the American Mission were, by the Divine blessing, the means of the conversion of the late King, who personally associated with the American missionaries in making known the Gospel to his people; and there have been thousands of others who, by means of their instrumentality, have built, and who still build their hopes of salvation on the Lord Jesus Christ. This is the best evidence that the American Mission has been no failure.

Letters, morals, external improvement, commerce, justice, and even liberty itself, are all highly valued by the missionary, but his chief object is the conversion of the soul to Christ. It is by the extent to which there is reason to hope that this has been accomplished that the degree of his success is to be determined. And that success is not to be measured by the standard of Christian attainment in countries where Christianity has existed for centuries, but by the standard of the churches in apostolic times, and by Mission churches in the heathen countries in the present day.

In reference to the estimation in which the missionaries are held, Mr. Dana, an American Episcopalian, bears the following testimony:

"I visited among all classes—the foreign merchants, traders, and shipmasters, foreign and native officials, and with the natives, from the King and several of the chiefs to the humblest poor, whom I saw without constraint in a tour I made alone over Hawaii, throwing myself upon their hospitality in their huts. I sought information from all, foreign and native, friendly and unfriendly; and the conclusion to which I came is, that the best men, and those who are best acquainted with the history of things here, hold in high esteem the labors and conduct of the missionaries."*

Another evidence of something more than mere surface Christianity is, among the Hawaiian Christians, most satisfactory. I refer to their liberality towards benevolent and religious objects. Their means are seldom abundant. The claims which the progress of society urge, increase with their advancement; nevertheless, from the forty churches

---

* Mr. R. H. Dana has, since the publication of Dr. Anderson's account, expressed his entire approval of the use the latter has made of his testimony in favor of the American missionaries.

connected with Mission stations, the contributions towards objects connected with the Mission, amounted in 1865, to $16,775, or £3,345.*

After these facts and figures we are warranted in saying that the annals of modern Missions do not contain a single instance of any body of Christian men proposing to send a Mission to a country where so large a proportion of the people were able to read and write, and where one-fourth of the population were church members, and three-fourths more or less connected with Christian congregations, even though some might have relapsed, or the Christian attainments of the best might be inferior to those of older communities.

SPECIAL REASONS ASSIGNED FOR COMMENCING A NEW MISSION.

Some of the special reasons assigned for commencing this Mission are remarkable. They are not grounded on the ignorance of the people, nor on their destitution of teachers, nor the unscriptural character of the preaching, for, in the opinion of their accusers, it is too closely scriptural. One charge against the American missionaries is, that they do not add something to what the Bible teaches, which the new Mission is to supply. This so called deficiency is said to prove that the Reformed Catholic Mission was required to save the remnant of the people from destruction, since the teaching of the Puritans has not sufficed to stop " the rapid and fearful diminution of the people."† The decrease of population since the discovery by Cook is a mournful fact, which no philanthropist can view without unfeigned sorrow. To ascribe its continued operation, though at a diminished rate, to the inefficiency of the teaching of the missionaries, when the influence of that teaching may justly be regarded as one of the chief agencies which Divine Providence has employed to save the race from annihilation, is wantonly to inflict no ordinary wrong.

Captain Cook's estimate of the population of Hawaii was probably too high, but there is no other extant. He calculated the population to be 400,000. Forty-four years afterwards, actual visitation to the chief inhabited parts of the Islands showed that the population had been reduced to about 130,000, so that the diminution had proceeded during that period at the rate of about 65 per cent. For the next thirty years, the de-

---
* American Society's Report for 1865.
† " Colonial Church Chronicle," p. 16, 1865.

crease, as shown by the census of the Government, was at the rate of 49 per cent. But for the seven years before the last Government census, the diminution of the population was only about 5 per cent., and it is hoped the next census will show at least a stationary population.* The subject is painfully interesting on many accounts, but its discussion would be unsuitable here ; and though an annual decrease of even five in every hundred of the people is not encouraging, yet contrasted with the decrease during the thirty-three years after the arrival of the Mission, it is evidence of the arresting and healing influence of the Gospel, which ought to have secured the teaching of the missionaries from censure, if it did not obtain acknowledgment and commendation.

I have endeavored to show that the reasons assigned for sending the Bishop and the Mission to Hawaii neither necessitated its appointment, nor justify the interference with the labors of the American Mission, and I have adduced counter testimony to show that, instead of being a failure, its success has at least equalled that of the most favored Missions in other parts of the world.

It has been charged against the missionaries that they have not restrained the immoralities of the people. That a degree of immorality still exists is admitted, and has never been denied. The missionaries know, to their mournful disappointment and sorrow, that it exists, and at some times and places more than at others. They know this, and truthfully report it. They mourn over it, and use every effort to reclaim its victims from ruin, often, by God's blessing, with success. But the existence of immorality in so recently organized a state of society, and with antecedents such as those of the Sandwich Islanders, is no proof of the failure of the Mission. As well might the crimes and vices of our own country, especially such as prevail in our seaports and large cities, occasionally in fearful proximity to our places of worship, be adduced as evidence that the centuries of Christian institutions and Christian teaching which England has enjoyed, have failed.

It is even asserted—most unjustly, inconsiderately, and mistakenly—by Bishop Staley, that immorality is in Hawaii ten times greater now than when the people were heathen. This is a monstrously absurd assertion. Not only is no evidence given to sustain it, but in the nature of things it is impossible that it should be so. Those who make this

---

* Anderson's "Hawaiian Islands," p. 271.

charge cannot know what the immorality of the heathen state was, and those who do know cannot declare it. It cannot be true ; for to say nothing of Christianity, there are other counteracting influences in the advance of civilization, education, commerce, and the influx of respectable foreign families, all which render it impossible that a worse state of morals should exist than that which prevailed under the savage, demoralizing and brutalizing reign of paganism.

It has been also affirmed that the teaching of the missionaries makes the people hypocrites, fostering unreality in religion, and that they have removed "the eternal landmarks between morality and immorality, teaching them that things innocent, like things wicked, were to be condemned." When and where, it may be asked, have they done this? Are heathen dances innocent things? Is there no immorality in the gambling invariably associated with their games? The "stern Puritanism," &c., of former times in America, caricatured and needlessly introduced into this discussion, has nothing to do with the question ; for the missionaries never taught the things mentioned. Puritanism is counted an honor by other Christians besides the American missionaries; and Calvinism,* which seems to be so offensive to the impugners of the Mission, finds a place in other articles of doctrine besides those of New England preachers. It is perhaps doubtful whether Bishop Staley, who pronounces so confidently upon the baneful influence of the preaching of the missionaries, ever heard one of their sermons, or even received a faithful report of one.

Even this charge against the missionaries of preaching the stern doctrines of Puritanism is only an ancient accusation revived to meet a modern necessity—the necessity of finding a reason for sending the new Mission to Honolulu. This charge was preferred and refuted forty years ago. In 1827, Captain Sayre, a gentleman of intelligence and observation, who had made two voyages to the Pacific and visited the Islands in both, spent several weeks on shore, conversed frequently with the Governor of Hawaii, took great pains to ascertain what was the char-

---

* Calvinism needs no vindication from me. But in a recent notice of the "Life of Robertson," in the "Theological Review," January, 1866, I find the subjoined reference to this subject : "Calvinism has had its heroic age—the age of the Pilgrim Fathers. It has a phase of heroism still, as many a bed of agonizing disease can testify, in home and hospital in England to-day." I have no sympathy with the tenets of which this Review is said to be an advocate ; but I can admire the nobility of mind which can look beyond the circle within which its own religious creed is enclosed, and behold good, and commend it when seen beyond that circle.

acter and conduct of the missionaries, and his testimony published on his return is, that their conduct was "firm, dignified, Christian, and moderate;" and that instead of, as had been stated, "attempting to force the darkest and most dreary parts of Puritan discipline upon the simple-minded Islanders, they instructed them in the plain, simple, practical truths and principles of the Gospel."*

I was myself associated with the first missionaries in their preaching labors, and never noticed anything contrary to the doctrines generally held by the Evangelical portion of Christendom. We often conferred together on the parts of Divine revelation most suitable to the peculiar state of the people. Three points we felt should be plainly and constantly set before them, viz., the consequences of sin, the necessity of regeneration to salvation, and the love and power of God in providing the means for securing both. Some of the missionaries thought that in the actual state of the people these truths should find a place in every address. In reference to my own teaching, I considered that every address might be the first and the last which some one would ever hear; for there were often very aged persons present, and I never considered that I had faithfully delivered the Gospel message unless, whatever might be my text, I had stated as plainly as I could that the wages of sin is death, that the gift of God is eternal life through Jesus Christ our Lord, and that he that believeth shall be saved.

The teaching of the other missionaries differed little from my own; and I only state this as evidence of what the teaching of the missionaries was at the close of 1824. There is no reason to suppose that it has changed on any material points since that time; some of my fellow-laborers are preachers there still; and I see no deviation from the doctrines then held in the books they have published at Honolulu, of some of which they have sent me copies.

The first book published by the missionaries, after the spelling book, was the Sermon on the Mount. The next was the History of Joseph. Thus far, there is certainly nothing to coerce the people by its severity into immorality; and authentic testimony to a different kind of teaching has yet to be adduced.

---
* Sag Harbor "Watchman," June 9, 1827.

THE TEACHING AND PRACTICE OF THE REFORMED CATHOLIC MISSIONARIES FRAUGHT WITH DANGER.

Having endeavored to show that the new Mission was not required by the circumstances of the people, and that the American Mission has been a remarkable success, I proceed to consider the nature of the remedy which those who condemn this previously existing and long-established Mission would themselves apply. In addition to the Holy Scriptures and to the Divine and ever-blessed Saviour, the new Mission proposes to introduce a branch of the Church which, according to the teaching of the new Mission, claims to be endowed with full and extraordinary apostolic power, and to constitute the sole medium through which the fullness of Divine love can be experienced by mankind. Bishop Staley states that the teaching of his Church is based on Scripture, not as it is by itself, and as it was given by inspiration of God, but as interpreted by the Fathers of the first five centuries. It is also stated that "the fullness of God's love, and the assurance of Christ's presence, can only be tasted through that one visible body the Church." It is therefore the branch or section of the Church of England which teaches these things that is proposed to be substituted for the Presbyterianism and Congregationalism of America.

So far as is apparent, either from the declarations or the proceedings of the Reformed Catholic missionaries, extreme ritualism, plenitude of apostolic power, and lenient church discipline, constitute, beyond the teaching of the Bible, the panacea for the remaining unexorcised heathen belief, for the immoralities, and the wasting decline of the population of the Sandwich Islands.

The simple introduction of the Episcopal form of worship with the teaching of what are generally regarded as the great essential doctrines of the Gospel at Honolulu, without baptismal regeneration or sacramental efficacy, would probably produce but trifling differences among the people; but the introduction of the teaching of peculiar doctrines connected with extreme ritualism, and "plenary apostolic power," especially baptismal regeneration, appears to me, and perhaps to many others besides, more likely to do harm than good; and I proceed to show my reasons for this opinion.

The first and most disastrous is, the tendency of this teaching and these practices to loosen and unsettle the foundations of all religious belief among the people. The faith of the Hawaiians is built simply and solely upon the Bible—the Word of God, as declared or contained in the Holy Scriptures. That is believed by them to be as the great teacher of the Gentiles declares "able to make wise unto salvation, through faith which is in Christ Jesus."*

Now Bishop Staley tells the Hawaiians, in his first sermon, that the worship of his Church is regulated by Holy Scripture, "as *it has been interpreted by the ancient Fathers;*" and further he affirms, if the statement already cited be correct, that the Hawaiians do not possess that "historical and common information which alone can render its perusal profitable or even safe." Here the utterance of Holy Scripture, given by the inspiration of God, and the words of the Bishop of Honolulu, are directly opposed to each other. The apostle Paul, writing, under Divine inspiration, to Timothy, declares that the Holy Scriptures are "able to make wise unto salvation." The Bishop affirms that the addition of "historical and common information can alone render their perusal profitable or even safe." This virtual denial of the sufficiency of Scripture to make wise unto salvation, cannot but unsettle the foundations of Hawaiian faith, especially if we consider the deficiencies of which the Bishop complains in the teaching previously given to aid them in their understanding of the Bible; for he says, "no attempt seems to have been made to teach them how to distinguish the human from the Divine, in the inspired volume."

In the present condition of the Hawaiians, so recently emerged from barbarism, so morally and intellectually immature and feeble, having already to resist the encroachments of the Romanists, who are active and untiring in their efforts to undermine this faith, their position is sufficiently critical. To introduce now any doubt respecting the sufficiency of Scripture alone, to teach all things necessary to salvation, would be like putting a mischievous weapon into the hands of the Romanist teachers, with which to defend their dogma of papal infallibility and authority, as alone able, and at the same time necessary, to decide all such questions. Under these circumstances, the very complaint that the Hawaiians have not been taught how to distinguish the Human from the Divine in the Bible will, in the opinion of all who reflect on the tendency

* 2 Tim. iii. 15.

of such speculations, among a community like the Hawaiians, appear to be a strong reason why the American missionaries should not be interfered with, much less supplanted, by those who would impart such teaching.

The great difference between the foundation of faith, as presented by the Bible, and the teaching set forth by Bishop Staley, in relation to both Sacraments—viz., regeneration by Baptism, and the Sacramental Grace connected with the Lord's Supper—and to some of the great doctrines of salvation, cannot but tend to lower the estimation in which the people now hold Divine revelation, and to disturb and weaken their newly implanted faith, which rests on the Word of God alone.

I pronounce no opinion on the ritualism which characterizes the proceedings of the Reformed Catholic Mission; but feel it my duty to state that, so far as I have observed or heard, all such appeals to the eye and to the senses, in such a state of society, produce impressions unfavorable to the growth of religion in the heart. The minds of people in a state corresponding with that of the Hawaiians, cannot perceive the spiritual meaning of such accompaniments of Christian worship; their minds are not refined or advanced sufficiently to appreciate their æsthetic influence, or understand anything beyond the appeals thus made to their senses. These additions may gratify their love of novelty and ornament, but they do not associate them with that spiritual reality and power over the heart and conscience, which they are accustomed to regard as belonging to the Word of God.

Accompaniments of this kind they invariably associate with their abandoned heathen worship, or the services connected with their idols, which, attended by peculiarly robed priests, were carried in processions, and whose worship was associated with gesticulations, bowings, prostrations, and silent mysterious movements. This has been, and is, the impression produced on the people of Tahiti, of Hawaii, and Madagascar, by the ceremonies of papal worship. They all said it was another kind of idol worship, resembling their own. At Hawaii, when the American missionaries pleaded with the rulers to treat gently the first Catholic priests, the chiefs answered: "What have we abolished idols for, if we are to allow that worship to be established here?"

I pronounce no opinion on the effect of extreme ritualism in more refined and cultivated communities who may be able to see a meaning and find a pleasure in such services; but among the Sandwich Islanders, these ceremonies are, in my most mature opinion, likely to produce more evil than good. They will tend to draw away the too easily diverted attention of the people from the spiritual engagements of religious worship, for "God is a Spirit," and His worship should be "in spirit and in truth;" to diminish the power of Divine truth on their consciences; and to intercept those direct and Divine communications to the soul, which Christians have ever found so enlightening to their understanding, so strengthening to their faith, and so cheering to their souls.

I must add that I am unable to conceive of any way in which the teaching or ritualism of the Reformed Catholic missionaries can diminish the immorality which the labors and influence and sufferings of the American Mission have been unable altogether to prevent. If the scriptural declaration of the consequences of sin, of the efficacy of the blood of Christ to cleanse from all sin, of the power of the Holy Spirit to regenerate the heart, of the willingness of our blessed Lord to receive all who come to Him, and the hope of eternal life which Holy Scripture unfolds to all who give evidence of the sincerity of their faith by an active holy life, be insufficient to enable the soul to turn from easily-besetting sin unto holiness and God, I cannot conceive how any ritualistic additions of candles and vestments and flowers, &c., or the interpretations of the ancient Fathers added to the inspired writings should accomplish this, or tend to save the remnant of the people from destruction. It is the "word of God," which is "the sword of the Spirit."* It is "the fear of the Lord" that "tendeth to life."†

I have never, since I left them, lost my interest in the religious progress of the Sandwich Islanders. I am still deeply concerned for their spiritual welfare. I have examined, with all the attention I have been able to give, the means proposed by the new Mission for removing the causes of regret and sorrow which to some extent are admitted to exist; and I am compelled to conclude, for the reasons above stated, that the remedies proposed are not calculated to diminish the existing evils, or to effect greater good than has been accomplished by the simpler and more scriptural teaching of the American missionaries.

* Ephes. vi. 17. † Prov. xix. 23.

A DIVINE LAW OF CHRIST DISREGARDED.

The Sandwich Islands as a field for missionary labor remained unoccupied by any other Christian teachers at the time when the American Society commenced its work there. That work it has continued for nearly fifty years, in the course of which it has sent out forty clerical missionaries, six physicians, twenty lay brethren, besides the wives of the missionaries and other female assistants. On that field it has expended more than two hundred thousand pounds of its resources. The great Head of the Church has already granted to its efforts encouraging success, with a prospect of still more satisfactory results. To the field thus effectively occupied, the projectors of the new Mission, instead of meeting an acknowledged want by sending, in compliance with the request of members of their own communion, a clergyman to "break to them the bread of life," have sent forth a Bishop with three clergymen, and propose to send three more. In thus intruding themselves upon a field on which the American Society had bestowed such ample, successful, and persevering labor, the Reformed Catholic Mission seem to have acted in utter forgetfulness, or else in entire disregard, of the just and equitable law of Christ, which enjoins on all Christians to "do unto others as they would that others should do unto them."

Had the American Missionary Society entered in a similar manner a field which the projectors of the new Mission had occupied with equal benefit to the people for forty years, every Protestant community in Christendom would have cried out against the violation of the explicit command of Christ, and, as it would appear to them, against the manifestation of that want of unity or oneness with other Christians which our Lord himself prayed might be the proof of His disciples' union with Himself, and the evidence to the world that His mission was Divine.*

Besides this, the teachings of experience, and the results of deep and prayerful reflection, have brought almost all Protestants engaged in this great work to consider it of the utmost importance to abstain from all intrusion upon fields already occupied by other Protestant missionaries. There is no authoritatively enjoined law on the subject; but this rule has so entirely commended itself to the judgment and right Christian feeling of all who have been engaged in directing missionary efforts that,

* John xvii. 21.

with scarcely more than a single exception, it has been almost invariably acted upon.

The Bishop of London thus alludes to this law of amity in his speech at Wells, on the occasion of Queen Emma's visit to that city : " It has been urged that there is a general law of amity in these matters which should prevent any missionary body from trespassing upon the fields of labor of others—a law which I fully recognize, because I feel that heathenism is wide enough, and there is room for all, without interfering with one another, to labor in some different portion of the field."

With the exception of perhaps one Society, all the Protestant missionary bodies in Europe, and, so far as I have heard, in America, engaged in modern Missions, on entering new fields of labor, or on occasions requiring its observance, have voluntarily and unhesitatingly respected this law of amity. The following may be regarded as instances of this:

In 1824, when the London Missionary Society appointed a colleague to join me in the Sandwich Islands, the secretary thus wrote :—" In coming to this determination, the directors by no means wished in the least to interfere with the arrangements of the American Society; and it was particularly specified in their resolution on the subject, that, provided it should not be perfectly in accordance with the sentiments and feelings of the worthy brethren of that Society, that Mr. Pitman should unite with them and you in the labors of the Sandwich Mission, he should, in that case, avail himself of the first opportunity which might occur to proceed to some other station."

I had been solicited by the King, the chiefs and missionaries to unite with the latter ; but when on my way to England I reached America, the officers of the American Board with whom I conferred appearing to think that, upon the whole, it would best promote the spread of the Gospel in that part of the world if they occupied the North Pacific, and the English missionaries the South, I expressed my concurrence in this opinion, reported the views of the American Board to the Directors in London, and the Mission to Hawaii was not resumed by that Society.

In the year 1830, the late Mr. Williams and Mr. Barff arranged with the Wesleyan missionaries at Tonga, the largest of the Friendly Islands, that the London Society should direct its efforts to Samoa and the Western Islands, while the Wesleyan Society should extend its labors to Fiji in the East. This arrangement was confirmed by the respective societies at home.

Before, however, the missionaries sent out from England by the former Society reached Samoa, two Wesleyan missionaries, having been invited from Tonga, had proceeded to those islands. The Directors of the London Missionary Society communicated the fact to the Wesleyan Society, who at once stated that the step had been taken without their knowledge, and again declared their intention to adhere to the arrangement already made. In their resolution on this subject, the Wesleyan Committee, in December, 1837, instructed their missionaries to withdraw, assigning the following as their reasons : " That in the fear of God, and in obedience to those principles of unchangeable equity and fair dealing, and of Christian brotherhood and union, which ought to regulate, in such cases, the conduct of kindred societies towards each other, they now deliberately confirm and renew their former decision on this question, as being, in their judgment, under all the circumstances, both right and fitting in itself, and, eventually, most likely to promote, on a large and general scale, the evangelization of the heathen population of the Polynesian Islands, and the peace and edification of the infant churches already established."*

In 1835, the Rev. C. T. E. Rhenius, a Lutheran clergyman, and several of his countrymen, who had occupied important stations under the Church Missionary Society in Tinnevelly, having, though continuing their labors in that Province, separated from the Church Society, proposed to unite themselves with the London Society, which had long occupied the adjacent province of Travancore. The London Society, considering the great discouragement and injury which such a proceeding would inflict on the operations of the Church Society, declined to receive these missionaries while they continued where they were, and only consented to accept their services in any of the stations remote from Tinnevelly at which the Tamil language was spoken. One of these brethren removed to a distant station under the care of the London Society, and the others, after the death of Rhenius, rejoined the Church Missionary Society, the peaceful course of whose proceedings in that important province has not since been disturbed.

I have adduced these instances to show the value of this voluntarily adopted law of amity in remedying 'evils which have threatened missionary operations abroad. It has been found to be equally beneficial at

* Records of London Missionary Society.

home. From the beginning, the directors of missionary effort have been accustomed to consider as sacred the field of labor occupied by others, when selecting or enlarging their own. The advantages are so self-evident, the practice so accordant with apostolic precept and conduct, as well as so congenial with the experience of the best fruits of the Spirit,* that the instances are extremely few amongst the Protestant communities, who have engaged in foreign Missions, in which it has been disregarded.

It was after conference with the London Society that the Scottish Society united with the former, and sent out its first missionaries to the Foulahs, in Western Africa; that the Netherlands Society commenced its first Mission at the Cape of Good Hope; and, more recently, that the Presbyterians of Nova Scotia commenced their Mission in the New Hebrides. It was after conference and correspondence with the London Society that the Paris Society sent out its first Mission to the Basoutous, in South Africa; and after conference or correspondence, most of the German modern Evangelical Missionary Societies have commenced their labors. It was after conference between the Bishop of Mauritius and myself on the spot, that an engagement was entered into on behalf of the Societies which we represented, that the London Missionary Society should continue to occupy the central part of Madagascar, and that the Societies of the Church of England should commence their labors among the tribes on the coast, and gradually work towards the interior, while we should extend our efforts towards the coast until we should meet. This arrangement was acquiesced in by the respective Societies at home; and it was in conformity therewith that the London Society declined to strengthen its station at Tamatave, which has been occupied by missionaries of the Society for the Propagation of the Gospel, while the Church Missionary Society selected its position on the northern coast. The American Missionary Society has also uniformly acted on the system of non-interference with other laborers in all the great fields of usefulness upon which it has entered. The instances are rare indeed, excepting in the great centres of civilization or commerce, in which it is necessary or desirable for the agents of two societies to occupy one field.

The officers of the Missionary Societies, the seat of whose operations is in London, have for many years past been accustomed to meet monthly

---
* Gal. v. 22, 23.

for conference and prayer in relation to their common work. On these occasions, the Secretaries of the Church, the Moravian, Wesleyan, Baptist and London Missionary Societies have often received valuable information and encouragement from each other at these friendly gatherings. There is also reason to believe that this intercourse has done much to extend and strengthen that broad catholic feeling in relation to the efforts of all Protestant Missions, which now so generally and so happily prevails.

By all those who cherish these feelings, the sending forth and continuing or extending the new Mission to the Sandwich Islands will be regarded, not only with extreme regret, but with serious apprehension. It cannot promote peace, brotherly kindness, or charity; and, besides the graver evils already apparent, it must tend to stir up vexatious rivalries, strife, and much evil work. It is doing so already, and so far as the interests of the Redeemer's kingdom among men, and the salvation of the souls of the Hawaiians are concerned, it holds out the promise of no compensating good, either to the Islanders, or to the patrons of the Mission.

This scheme, as the Bishop of London stated at Wells, did not originate with his lordship, nor with the late venerable Archbishop of Canterbury, but with certain members of the Church of England, and when the adherents of that or of any other church chose to enter upon such a course no one questioned their perfect right to do so; but the expediency or advantage of such a course may, nevertheless, be extremely questionable, and when another society has, with great expenditure of life and means, long cultivated any field, in the hope of reaping not temporal benefits, but the satisfaction and the welcome enjoyment which success in winning souls for Christ affords, the invasion of this field, the appropriation of these fruits, is neither a position nor an occupation in which the best friends of the Church of England, will consider her children either most appropriately or honorably employed.

The Supreme Ruler of the world seems by the events of his Providence, to be giving us India, and opening to us China and Africa, as well as other parts of Asia; to be calling the varied sections of His Church to the great work of turning the nations of the earth from dumb idols to serve the living God. Among the bands of faithful men which the churches are sending forth to this work, the venerable antiquity, the exalted rank, the vast resources, which belong to the Church of England, and the dauntless courage which the adherents of that Church have inscribed on the page of our nation's history, point out the front ranks, the high places of the field, where the difficulties are the most formidable, and the struggle most arduous, as the position which belongs to the Church of England, and which her sons would most appropriately occupy. That Church neither does justice to herself, nor achieves all the good that she might in the world, with such wide and transcendantly glorious prospects before her, by using any part of her great resources and influence in following the march of others who have broken the ranks of the enemy, and gathering up the spoils of a field which they have already won.

Not only does the new Mission to the Sandwich Islands fail to encourage other laborers in the great enterprise, but its persistent continuance will seem to threaten with disappointment and injury all other missionaries besides.

If after the labor and resources which, during forty years, the American Society has devoted to the Sandwich Islands, and the gratifying results which, after all needful deductions, have most certainly been attained, the simple circumstance of the King of the country and a few members of the English and American Episcopal Church, asking that a clergyman may be sent out to them, be deemed a sufficient reason for sending out a Bishop and a Mission of several clergymen to be joined by others from America, not to minister to the members of their own respective churches, but to spread themselves among the general population, for whose spiritual good the American missionaries have been so long laboring, to draw them away from these teachers and their simple faith, other Missions may expect similar treatment. What encouragement, it may be asked, has any missionary body, European or American, to expect to be allowed peacefully and rightfully to reap the fruits of their own efforts ? What ground has any missionary body to conclude, after long and faithful labor, that the members of the Reformed Catholic Committee, or other persons who may think their own mode of worship or its accompaniments better or likely to be more agreeable to the people than that already introduced, may not, unrestrained by any law of amity, and disregarding the great and universal law of Christ, deem themselves justified in condemning the work already accomplished as producing only a surface religion, and sending forth their own agents to draw away the converts from those who had long watched for their souls, to their own creed and worship?

The Bishop of London, with that characteristic benevolence which moves him to look on the most favorable side of occurrences connected with the progress of Christianity, expressed a hope that the union of the Episcopal Church in America with this Mission would prove an olive branch; but it is to be feared that the reverse will be the case. The American Society is not a circumscribed association, extemporized, as it were, yesterday, but one of the earliest, most widely extended, highly esteemed, and liberally supported organizations of the kind in America.* The high character of its agents, and the benefits they have conferred on different portions of mankind, are acknowledged by the friends of all other Protestant Missions. The missionaries in the Sandwich Islands are members of that sacred brotherhood which has proved so efficient in India, China and Western Asia, and whom the Turkish Aid Society in England, supported among others by such distinguished philanthropists as Sir John Lawrence, and the late Archbishop of Dublin, has so generously assisted in their great and holy work.

The supporters of the American Society all know that during the long forty years that their missionaries prosecuted their work under many difficulties and privations, the Episcopalians in America manifested no interest whatever in Hawaii, and the invitation of the Reformed Catholic Committee to the American Episcopalians to join them now will produce no good feeling, but the reverse. It will increase the sense of gratuitous injury and wrong should the proceedings of these parties damage the American Mission in the Sandwich Islands.

Disasters, it is to be feared, arising out of this intrusion, are beginning to appear in the Islands; changes are apprehended in the religious teaching in the common schools; and the increase of the Reformed Catholic missionaries is being regarded as a political as well as an ecclesiastical invasion. I do not regard it as such, but we cannot wonder that the Americans, who form the chief part of the foreign residents, should do so.

* * * * * * * * * *

---

* The resources of this Society are contributed by residents in the States of the Union known as constituting the North. It is supported by 2,840 Congregational churches, containing 269,000 communicants, and 1,479 New School Presbyterian churches, with 143,000 members, altogether 4,319 churches, containing 412,000 communicants. Its income last year amounted to £111,469, and the number of ordained missionaries was 143.

I shall now conclude by adducing two living witnesses of the fruits of the labors of the American missionaries, to which both England and America have borne indisputable testimony, as my last reasons why the American missionaries should be no further interfered with.

The following account of a sermon preached at Christ Church, Clapham, by the Rev. W. Hoapili, was copied from the London " Times " into a Sandwich Island newspaper of November 17th, 1865. After noticing the ritualism of the service, the "Times" continues : "At the end of the Nicene Creed, which was very chastely and beautifully sung, the Rev. W. Hoapili ascended the pulpit, wearing his surplice, with his stole crossed over his left shoulder, indicating that he had not yet advanced beyond deacon's orders in the Church. He is a tall, dark, handsome young man, wearing a beard and moustache, and with so slight a foreign accent that it was scarcely possible to detect he was not an Englishman."

The editor of the " Pacific Commercial Advertiser " observes : " Our object in quoting these paragraphs is merely to bring before the minds of our readers the tribute which is therein paid to the literary and educational system of instruction of the American missionaries on the Hawaiian Islands. We are confident that the Rev. W. Hoapili never went one day to any school except to those taught by or instituted by the American missionaries, and yet the young man speaks the English language so accurately that ' it was scarcely possible to detect that he was not an Englishman.' Now, we are bold to assert that there are scores— ay, hundreds—of young Hawaiians, as well, if not better, educated than Mr. Hoapili. Whatever American missionaries may have neglected to do, they certainly have not neglected to give Hawaiian youth such an education as the youth of but few nations can boast. There are undisguised attempts on the part of some to ignore these facts, and they are laboring with a zeal ' worthy of a better cause ' to produce the impression that the American Mission at these Islands is a failure. Never was there a greater falsification of facts or perversion of the truth. It is morally wrong that such a view should be imparted to the history of our times and the Hawaiian nation, and those who attempt to do so are surely enemies of the nation. Napoleon, the Emperor of France, asserts, in the opening paragraph to his ' History of Julius Cæsar,' that ' Historic truth ought to be no less sacred than religion.' "

The second instance of the efficiency of the teaching of the American missionaries is from a native missionary pastor, sent by the Hawaiian native church to a distant heathen race. It is copied from an American journal, the "Christian Register,' of March 3d, 1866. The introduction was written by an honorable and candid gentleman, who is a native of Boston, but who has spent twelve years in the Sandwich Islands, acting part of that time as a judge. His religious associations are not those of the missionaries; his testimony is therefore the more reliable, and will speak for itself.

"In 1853 Matunui, a Chief of the Marquesas or Nuuhiva Islands, came to the Sandwich Islands to beg that Missionaries might be sent to his native group. He had heard of the benefits which the Sandwich Islands had derived from the introduction of civilization and Christianity, (which to his mind seem to have been synonymous,) and he wished that he and his people might partake of them. Such a call could not be disregarded; those of us who were most skeptical as to the wisdom of Foreign Missions generally, were ready to say God-speed to the little band that went out in answer to that call. They consisted of one white layman, unmarried, and two Hawaiian ministers, who took their wives with them.

"These native missionaries have remained at their post until now. Two years ago one of them was instrumental in saving the life of an American—the mate of a whaleship. Our Government sent to him some gifts in acknowledgment of the service. The following letter, written by this Missionary—Rev. James Kekela—on the receipt of those gifts, was received at Washington too late to meet the eye of the good President to whom it is addressed. I am sure its simple utterances would have delighted and touched that warm, loving heart. I have re-translated it. The translation which was received at the State Department, and which was made in Honolulu, is more elegant than this, but has sacrificed the native idiom, and, in some cases, the very spirit of the original, to smoothness of expression.

"I commend the letter to your readers. My translation fails of doing full justice to the original, yet I much mistake if they will not see in its expressions of faith and of love a beauty and power that could flow only from a life of entire consecration to God's service. This poor Sandwich Islander, whose grand-parents were just such dark, benighted cannibals as he is now laboring for, comes nearer in his spirit to the apostolic writers than many of our most learned Divines and Commentators.

"How admirably does this man's child-like story of his own life, and of his love to God and to his neighbor, refute those unworthy aspersions upon the labors and success of the American Missionaries at the Sandwich Islands, which we have so often heard. These aspersions have not been so often repeated here of late as they were formerly, but in England we find them uttered in various forms by the Bishop of Oxford and others, who have been striving to build up a rival Mission at those Islands, some of them moved, undoubtedly, by their zeal for their Church, others, as undoubtedly, moved by a desire to advance the political interests of Great Britain at the Islands at the expense of those of the United States, with a view to their ultimate occupation as a British naval station. Who shall dare deny that this man is in the true apostolic succession? Who in this age better than he represents the 'Apostle to the Gentiles?'" E. P. BOND."

[Translated expressly for the "Christian Register."]

"HIVAOA, March 27, 1865.

"*To A. Lincoln, President of the United States of America:*

"Greetings to you, great and good friend!

"My mind is stirred up to address you in friendship by the receipt of your communication through your Minister resident in Honolulu, James McBride.

"I greatly respect you for holding converse with such humble ones. Such you well know us to be.

"I am a native of the Hawaiian Islands, from Waialua, Oahu, born in 1824, and at twelve years of age attended the school, at Waialua, of Rev. Mr. Emerson; and was instructed in reading, writing, and mental arithmetic and geography.

"In 1838 I was entered at the High School of Lahainaluna, and was under the instruction of Messrs. L. Andrews, E. W. Clark, S. Dibble and Alexander. Not being in advance of others, I remained in the school some years, and in 1843 I graduated, and was then invited and desired by the teachers to continue my studies in other branches, that is, to join a class in theology under the Rev. S. Dibble. He died in 1845, and I and others continued the study of the Scriptures under

W. P. Alexander. In 1847 I graduated, having been at Lahainaluna nine years. In that year, 1847, I married a girl from my native place, who had for seven years attended a female seminary at Wailuku, under the instruction of J. S. Green, E. Bailey and Miss Ogden.

"In the same year, 1847, I and my wife were called to Kahuku, a remote place in Koolau, on Oahu, to instruct the people there in the Scriptures and other words of wisdom. I remained in this work for some years. It was clear to my wife and myself that our lives were not our own, but belonged to the Lord, and therefore we covenanted with one another that we would be the Lord's, 'His only, His forever.' And from that time forth we yielded ourselves servants unto the Lord. In 1852 certain American Missionaries—Dr. Gulick and others—were sent out on their way to Micronesia. I was one of their company, and, after seven months absence, I returned with E. W. Clark. On my return I was employed in arousing the Hawaiians to the work of Foreign Missions.

"In 1853 there came to our islands a Macedonian cry for Missionaries to Nuuhiva, brought by Matunui, a Chief of Fatuhiva.

"The Missionaries speedily laid hold upon me to go to this group of islands. I did not assent immediately. I stopped to consider carefully, with much prayer to God to make clear to me that this call was from God, and I took counsel with my wife. It was evident to us that this was a call from God, therefore we consented to come to these dark, benighted and cannibal islands.

"I had aged parents, and my wife beloved relatives, and we had a little girl three years old. We left them in our native land. We came away to seek the salvation of the souls of this people, because our hearts were full of the Love of God. This was the only ground of our coming hither, away from our native land.

"In the year 1853 we came to these cannibal islands, and we dwelt first for four years at Fatuhiva, and in 1857 we removed to Hivaoa, another island, to do the work of the Lord Jesus; and from that time until now we have striven to do the work of Jesus Chrst, without regard for wealth or worldly pleasure. We came for the Lord, to seek the salvation of men, and this is our only motive for remaining in this dark land.

"When I saw one of your countrymen, a citizen of your great nation, ill-treated, and about to be baked and eaten, as a pig is eaten, I ran to save him, full of pity and grief at the evil deed of these benighted people. I gave my boat for the stranger's life. This boat came from James Hunnewell,* a gift of friendship. It became the ransom of this countryman of yours, that he might not be eaten by the savages who knew not Jehovah. This was Mr. Whalon,† and the date January 14, 1864.

"As to this friendly deed of mine in saving Mr. Whalon, its seed came from your great land, and was brought by certain of your countrymen, who had received the love of God. It was planted in Hawaii, and I brought it to plant in this land and in these dark regions, that they might receive the root of all that is good and true, which is *love*.

"1. Love to Jehovah.
"2. Love to self.
"3. Love to our neighbor.

"If a man have a sufficiency of these three, he is good and holy, like his God, Jehovah, in His triune character, (Father, Son and Holy Ghost,) one-three, three-one. If he have two and wants one, it is not well; and if he have one and wants two, this, indeed, is not well; but if he cherishes all three, then he is holy, indeed, after the manner of the Bible.

"This is a great thing for your great nation to boast of before all the nations of the earth. From your great land a most precious seed was brought to the land of darkness. It was planted here, not by means of guns, and men-of-war, and threatenings. It was planted by means of the ignorant, the neglected, the despised. Such was the introduction of the word of the Almighty God into this group of Nuuhiva. Great is my debt to Americans, who have taught me all things pertaining to this life, and to that which is to come.

"How shall I repay your great kindness to me? Thus David asked of Jehovah, and thus I ask of you, the President of the United States. This is my only payment—that which I have received of the Lord— love (*aloha*.)

---

* I had frequent personal intercourse with this gentleman, who was engaged in mercantile pursuits when I resided at Oahu. He was an honorable Christian man, and it is a pleasure to find that he is still, as of old, encouraging the laborers in this distant Mission field.

† The seaman.

"I and my wife, Naomi, have five children, the first with Miss Ogden, the second with Rev. J. S. Emerson; we now send the third to live with Rev. L. H. Gulick; the fourth is with Kauwealoha, my fellow-Missionary, and the fifth is with us at present. Another stranger is soon expected. There is heaviness in thus having to scatter the children where they can be well taken care of.

" We have received your gifts of friendship according to your instructions to your Minister, James McBride. Ah! I greatly honor your interest in this countryman of yours. It is, indeed, in keeping with all I have known of your acts as President of the United States.

" A clear witness this in all lands of your love for those whose deeds are love, as saith the Scripture, ' Thou shalt love Jehovah, and shalt love thy neighbor as thyself.'

" And so may the love of the Lord Jesus abound with you until the end of this terrible war in your land.

" I am, Abraham Lincoln, President of the United States,
           " Your obedient servant,
    [Signed]   " JAMES KEKELA."

With this simple, ingenuous and truthful testimony to the ability and faithfulness with which the American missionaries have discharged their high and sacred duties to the Sandwich Islanders, I close my vindication of their characters and labors, and express my most earnest hope, as respectfully suggested by the American Board, in their letter to the Venerable Society for the Propagation of the Gospel, in November, 1864, that " upon a reconsideration of the case, in view of the facts now presented," that Society "will think it proper to withdraw from interference with our labors in the Sandwich Islands, which have been so signally blessed of God."

I also appeal most respectfully, sincerely and earnestly, as an Englishman, as an English missionary, not to the members of the Society for the Propagation of the Gospel only, but to the promoters of the new Mission, carefully to reconsider whether it would not, be far better for the interests of peace and of religion in the Sandwich Islands, and tend more to the Christian enlightenment of the heathen world, of which so large a portion still remains destitute of the knowledge of the Gospel. for them to make every needful provision for the wants of the members of the Episcopal Church in Honolulu, and, in all beyond that, to leave the American missionaries to carry forward their own work without further interruption.

APPENDIX.

Note A.

Department of Foreign Affairs, City of Honolulu,
March 13th, 1860.

Sir :—I have the honor to enclose to you a sealed letter from the Rev. Richard Armstrong, D. D., President of the Board of Public Instruction, which, he informs me, is on the subject of the establishment, in this capital, of an Episcopal Church.

Their Majesties the King and Queen prefer that form of worship, and were married according to the rites of the English Episcopal Church.

The King himself, taking all the interest in the education, morals and religion of his people which becomes him as Sovereign, believes that an Episcopal Church here, besides supplying a want long felt by many British and American families, would operate beneficially in narrowing the existing broad antagonism of the Calvinistic and Catholic creeds, and thereby promote that brotherly feeling between the clergy of both that so well becomes the followers of the same Lord.

By orders of his Majesty, I have written fully upon this subject to Manly Hopkins, Esq., of 4, Royal Exchange Buildings, who is the King's Charge d'Affaires and Consul-General in London. If you honor him with a call, he will communicate to you what farther information you may desire. **Bancroft**

In the undersigned you may not recognize an old acquaintance. While on shore, on the 10th of May, 1824, (I being then on my voyage to Calcutta in my yacht, the "Daule,") I had the honor to be introduced to you and to your good lady by Mr. Crocker, then acting as Consul of the United States; and, favored with your company, I visited a native school, and heard the scholars repeat the Lord's Prayer in the Hawaiian language.
I have the honor to be,
Rev. Sir,
Your most obedient, humble servant,
R. C. Wyllie.

Rev. William Ellis.

HONOLULU, SANDWICH ISLANDS,
February 29th, 1860.

DEAR SIR:—Having been a resident of this place many years ago, your name being yet fresh in the recollection of many here, both native and foreign, you will be prepared to appreciate the object of this letter, and I will therefore make no apology for addressing it to you.

Besides the two large native churches we have here, two of the Congregational order (one of them in connection with the Seaman's Chapel, and one Methodist, neither of them large; for our foreign population is small, except in the whaling season, when foreign ships resort to our ports,) there are quite a number of persons here, and a few families, who are either members of the Episcopal Church, or partial to that Church, and they have long been desirous to secure the services of an Episcopal minister to break to them the bread of life. Several months ago the King, who takes much interest in the subject, directed his Minister of Foreign Relations, R. C. Wyllie, a gentleman from Scotland, who also feels great interest in the matter, to write to Manly Hopkins, Esq., H. H. M.'s Charge d'Affaires in London, authorizing him to guarantee to a suitable clergyman of the Episcopalian Church who may come to Honolulu, and labor for the spiritual good of its population, an annual salary of one thousand dollars, hoping that a full salary might be made up for him by this, and what might be contributed for the object in England. Less than two thousand dollars would be insufficient. And should the right man be obtained, he will have no difficulty in raising this amount here. The King has offered a lot of ground as a site for an Episcopal Church, and there will, I think, be no difficulty in raising means here to erect one upon it.

How to obtain just the *right man* is a question of great interest, not only to those of the Episcopal Church, but to all who love Zion here; and here is just the reason for the liberty I have taken in addressing you now. You have lived here, have associated with American missionaries, (of whom I was one for sixteen years, and for eleven years I have been honored with the charge of the department of Public Instruction,) and you would know at once what kind of a man would be calculated to do good here. I may add, also, that I address you at the request of several Episcopalians, who are among our best people. They want a man of Evangelical sentiments, of respectable talents, and most exemplary Christian life.

We are now enjoying for a few days the society of the Rev. Messrs. Garrett and Low, Episcopal clergymen from England, bound to British Columbia. With Mr. Garrett our people are greatly pleased, and would be glad to have him settled here, but he is under engagement to go on; and he strongly recommends a friend of his.

Would you be so kind as to inquire about this gentleman, and if satisfied of his qualifications, recommend him to the Bishop of London, and also to Manly Hopkins, Esq. Mr. Garrett thinks he would come, and is *just the man*. But, if not, could you see the Bishop of London on the subject, both in regard to a suitable man, and a portion of his support; though I think, if acceptable, he will very soon get his entire support here.

Not knowing your address, I will take the liberty to enclose this through my good friend Dr. Anderson, of Boston.

With sentiments of esteem and Christian regard,

I am, Sir,

Your obedient servant,

R. ARMSTRONG.

Rev. William Ellis.

P. S.—On reflection, I conclude to send this open through Mr. Wyllie, who will enclose it officially.

The following admirable review of this pamphlet from the London "Record" of April 25th, is inserted in this edition, though not in the original:

THE HAWAIIAN REFORMED CATHOLIC MISSION.

We have had occasion to refer more than once to the proceedings of "the Reformed Catholic Mission at Honolulu," and of Bishop Staley, who is at the head of it. We have strongly protested against this intrusion of members of our own church into a missionary sphere already occupied by another body of Christians, as an act at once unjust, uncourteous and unwise, as directly violating the mutual understanding on which the various sections of the church of Christ have hitherto conducted their missions, and contradicting alike apostolic precept and apostolic practice. It has been shown by us that the Church of England has ever recognized the various Reformed churches as being true churches of Christ, and worthy compeers with herself in the great work of evangelizing the world. We had, however, at that time, no conception that the case was so bad as it turns out to be. A pamphlet on this subject has just been issued by the Rev. W. Ellis, well known in connection with Madagascar, and formerly a missionary in the Sandwich Islands, and therefore possessing a personal acquaintance with the character and circumstances of the inhabitants. The high character of Mr. Ellis, united with his personal acquaintance with the facts, invest his defense of the American Missions and his grave charges against the originators of the Reformed Catholic Mission with equal authority and importance. It is scarcely possible that so well-furnished an author should be found tripping. Indeed every statement he makes is accompanied with evidence, and he writes moreover with a moderation of tone and spirit calculated to show that he is no heated and reckless partisan. And yet, unless his statements can be disproved or in some way rebutted, it will be impossible to avoid the conclusion that this Reformed Catholic Mission, whatever the name may mean, is one of the grossest delusions ever palmed upon Christian men.

The establishment of the Episcopal Mission at Honolulu was warmly advocated by some high churchmen on grounds apparently equally conclusive to the reason and touching to the sympathies. "A sort of historic and chivalrous charm was imparted to the enterprise by representing the non-compliance of the Government of England with a series of applications made by successive sovereigns of Hawaii as so many wrongs inflicted on the people which the Church of England is now called upon to redress." Twenty years after Captain Cook's visit, Vancouver brought religious truth before the mind of Kamehameha I., and promised him teachers from England. The fulfillment of this promise was pathetically urged by the King, but urged in vain. Thirty years later a similar application was made by Kamehameha II. and again refused, although the King visited England in person to press the application and to "take back with him an English Church establishment." The Hawaiians still continued to look "with an eager eye for the church of the future to be sent to them from England."

In 1857 the old desire again broke out in a request addressed by Kamehameha IV. to the Queen of England and the Archbishop of Canterbury that " a Mission of the Church of England should be sent out to Honolulu." Nothing less than a bishop and six clergymen would suffice to meet the wants of a population of 68,000 souls, of whom 20,000 only were professing Protestants and 25,000 unconnected with any creed. All that had before been done for this people had been done by "American Puritans," who had inflicted on a people addicted to gaiety and spending much of their life in the innocent recreation of the dance, the restrictions natural to " descendants of the stern old Puritans of New England, if anything rather more severe, sour and vinegar-like." These people had so grossly mismanaged their Missions that they " made hypocrites as fast as they made proselytes," producing " a superficial Christianity thinly veiling a heathen faith and heathen practices." They made the mistake of " introducing themselves into the secular offices of the Kingdom," and were so utterly powerless even to arrest the progress of heathen profligacy that " immorality in Hawaii is ten times greater now than when the people were heathen." Under such circumstances it is no wonder that " the people are craving for your teachers, that they are wearied out by the mismanagement of the American Puritans." Hence, lastly, the appeal—shall all this be in vain, and will not English Christians throw light on their Hawaiian darkness by establishing among them the Reformed Catholic Mission and erecting a new cathedral at Honolulu, that neglected place, where among a population of 14,000 souls there are only two churches, capable of containing 2,500 persons, two chapels and a Roman Catholic cathedral to boot?

Such is the statement put forth by those high churchmen who unlike the great Apostle, desired "to enter into other men's labors." It contains, as we have put it, fourteen direct statements of matters of fact; and if these statements were true, some ground for a new Mission would undoubtedly have existed. What will our readers think when we tell them that Mr. Ellis adduces strong grounds to show that every one of these fourteen statements is, without exception, simply and absolutely *untrue!* We do not profess to discuss the details. We only call attention to the results, unless the contents of the pamphlet can be disproved. But we cannot refrain from the strong indignation at the unseemly, gross and scandalous manner in which the American missionaries, than whom, as a class, no more devoted body of men exists, have been libellously attacked alike by the Bishop of Oxford and by Bishop Staley.

Of this gentleman's opinions and modes of proceeding our columns have contained illustrations on former occasions. Judging from the facts stated in Mr. Ellis's pamphlet, and supposing them to be true, he appears to be a theological hybrid, of a species unhappily not unknown in these later days, combining the narrowest bigotry of extreme high churchism with the doctrinal laxity of the school of Bishop Colenso. By virtue of the one-half of this theological compound, he appears to teach the co-ordinate authority of tradition with Scripture, baptismal regeneration and sacramental grace in connection with the Lord's Supper, and to give expression to his views in that "language of dogma," Anglican ritualism. By virtue of his other half, not once he calls into question the inspiration of Holy Scripture, distinguishing what is human in Scripture from what is Divine, (not, it will be observed, combining the two elements in one revelation, but dividing the one revelation into two parts,) "eternal principles from what is temporary and incidental." We transcribe the whole passage in the Bishop's own words: "They (the Hawaiians) have anything but an intelligent acquaintance with the Holy Scripture. Of its composite character, of the times and circumstances of the authors when they wrote the various books, they know nothing; they do not, in fact, possess that historical and common information which can alone render its perusal profitable and even safe. No attempt seems to have been made to teach them how to distinguish the human from the Divine in the Inspired Volume—eternal principles from what is temporary and incidental."

Every one who reads the pamphlet referred to in this article will feel that explanation is loudly called for from the friends of " the Reformed Catholic Mission." If the statements of Mr. Ellis can be rebutted by evidence on the other side, let it be done, but the reputation of all parties concerned demands that it should be done at once. Many excellent and high-minded persons have been led to support this Mission who are utterly incapable of knowingly lending themselves to any unworthy or ungenerous scheme. If Mr. Ellis be right, these men must have been grossly deceived. It is due to themselves to ascertain the facts, and vindicate their reputation from any share in what appears little better than a delusion. If this is not done, indelible disgrace will rest on all who do not separate themselves at once and for ever from a movement publicly convicted of being founded either on the most culpable ignorance or the grossest lack of truth.

www.ingramcontent.com/pod-product-compliance
Lightning Source LLC
Chambersburg PA
CBHW020337090426
42735CB00009B/1578